STECK-VAUGHN

Vocabulary Advantage

FOR

American History

Student Work Text

Vivian Bernstein

Steck
Vaughn™

A Harcourt Achieve Imprint

www.Steck-Vaughn.com
1-800-531-5015

Reading Level:	8 - 10
Category:	Instructional - Language
Subcategory:	Vocabulary/Skill Building
Workbook Available:	
Teacher Guide Available:	Yes
Part of a Series:	Yes
CD / CD ROM / DVD Available:	

Acknowledgements

Executive Editor	Eduardo Aparicio
Senior Editor	Victoria Davis
Design Team	Cindi Ellis, Cynthia Hannon, Jean O'Dette
Media Researchers	Nicole Mlakar, Stephanie Arsenault
Production Team	Mychael Ferris-Pacheco, Paula Schumann, Alia Hasan
Creative Team	Joan Cunningham, Alan Klemp

Photo Credits

Photo Credits: Pages 20, 26d, 32d, 44d, and 50d ©The Granger Collection, NY; p. 62d ©Bettmann/CORBIS; p. 68d ©The Granger Collection, NY; p. 80d ©Hulton Archive/Getty Images.

Additional photography by Comstock Royalty Free, Digital Vision/Getty Images Royalty Free, Eyewire/Getty Images Royalty Free, PhotoDisc/Getty Images Royalty Free, Photos.com Royalty Free, Reagan Bradshaw, Royalty-Free/CORBIS, and Thinkstock/Getty Images Royalty Free.

ISBN 1-4190-1920-1

© 2007 Harcourt Achieve Inc.

Steck-Vaughn is a trademark of Harcourt Achieve Inc.

Printed in the United States of America
3 4 5 6 7 8 9 0956 12 11 10 09

Dear Student,

Welcome to _Vocabulary Advantage for American History_!

In this Student Work Text, you will

- learn new history words that will help you better understand what you read in your history textbook,

- learn useful words that will help you in the classroom and on tests, and

- learn skills that will help you figure out the meaning of other new words.

You will write and talk about the new words you've learned. You should also feel free to draw, circle, underline, and make notes on the pages of this Work Text to help you remember what these words mean. You can do more writing and drawing in your American History Vocabulary Journal.

All of the tools in this book will help you build your own understanding of important history and classroom vocabulary. Building your understanding of these words will give you an advantage in your history class and on history tests!

Have fun!

Table of Contents

Read the passage below. Think about the meanings of the new words printed in **bold**. Underline any definitions that might help you figure out what the new words mean. The first one has been done for you.

Moving to America

Vocabulary Strategy

Writers will often place definitions of new or difficult words near those words in a text. Look for these definitions to help you understand the meanings of new words.

Who were the first Americans, and when did they begin living in North America? Scientists believe that thousands of years ago, there was a large **migration**, <u>or movement, of people</u> to America from Asia. Many scientists **speculate**, or <u>guess, that a land bridge existed long ago</u> between Asia and Alaska. They also believe that some people from Asia walked across the land bridge and then settled in different **regions**, or <u>areas, of North and South America.</u>

Scientists have learned a lot about the way the first Americans lived by studying their **artifacts**. These artifacts included tools and objects that were made by people. From these ancient artifacts, we now know that the earliest Americans built amazing **civilizations**, or developed ways of life, throughout the Americas.

 New American History Words

artifacts

   noun   tools and objects made by people

civilization

   noun   a group of people who share the same art, history and laws

migration

   noun   movement of people or animals from one area to another

region

   noun   a large area of similar land

Now read this passage and practice the vocabulary strategy again. Underline any definitions in the passage that might help you figure out what the new words in **bold** mean.

Learning to Live in North America

After crossing the land bridge, the first Americans slowly settled throughout North America. Today we call these first Americans the Native Americans. These Native Americans learned to use the **environment**, or the land, plants, and animals of where they lived, for food and shelter. Native Americans who lived in forests near the Pacific Ocean in the Northwest ate fish. They built homes from the trees in the forests. In **contrast** to Native Americans in the Northwest, Native Americans of the dry Southwest learned to farm. In other parts of North America, people learned to **domesticate**, or tame animals to help them grow food.

As time passed, people began to live together in groups called **societies**. Each society had its own laws, leaders, and its own way of life. Throughout North America, Native Americans developed different **cultures**. Today, different Native American groups continue to celebrate their languages, arts, dances, and customs.

More New American History Words

culture

noun   a body of shared traditions and beliefs

domesticate

verb   to tame animals and grow plants for human use

environment

noun   the land, plants, and animals in an area

society

noun   people who live together as a group and share laws and customs

I'm just **speculating**, but I think you are in the wrong **environment**.

Fishing Poles For Rent

Other Useful Words

contrast

noun   the differences between things

verb   to compare the differences between things

speculate

verb   to guess or to think about

Apply the Strategy

Look at a chapter in your textbook that your teacher identifies. Use definitions to help you figure out the meaning of any new words you find.

Matching

Finish the sentences in Group A with words from Group B. Write the letter of the word on the line. Discuss your choices with a partner.

Group A

1 Long ago there was a _____ of people from Asia to America.

2 Old pots, tools, and art from long ago are different types of _____.

3 A large area of similar land is called a _____.

4 The art, music, laws, and customs of people in America became new _____.

5 Since we did not see it happen, we can only _____ about how people migrated from Asia to North and South America.

Group B

A. civilizations

B. speculate

C. region

D. migration

E. artifacts

Group A

6 The dry Southwest had a different _____ than the rainy forests of the Northwest.

7 As people learned to farm, they _____ animals and plants for human use.

8 Native Americans formed groups, or _____ based on the culture and environment of where they lived.

9 There is a _____, or difference between the environment and way of life of America's Northwest and Southwest.

10 Native American _____ included art, music, songs, and language.

Group B

F. societies

G. contrast

H. environment

I. culture

J. domesticated

Word Challenge: What's Your Reason?

Take turns with a partner reading the statements below out loud. Think of a reason for each statement and write it on the line. Write your reasons in complete sentences. The first one has been done for you.

1 A **society** could not exist where there is no food or water. _People create societies and people must have food and water._

2 Tigers and lions should not be **domesticated**. _____

_____

3 There is a great **contrast** in the homes in a desert and the homes in a forest. _____

_____

4 I would enjoy visiting another **culture**. _____

_____

Word Challenge: What's Your Answer?

Take turns with a partner reading each question out loud and writing an answer on the line. Answer the questions with complete sentences. The first one has been done for you.

1 Why wouldn't you want to live far from all **civilizations**? _Civilizations have the art, education, and laws that people need._

2 Why should you protect the **environment**? _____

_____

3 What kind of **artifacts** show how people cooked and ate food? _____

_____

4 What kind of **region** would you like to migrate to? _____

_____

Finish the Sentence

Use a word from the box to finish each sentence. Write the correct word on the line. Discuss your choices with a partner.

migration	artifact	speculated	domesticated	region

1 Dogs were the first animals to be _____, or raised to live with people.

2 We _____ about who might have taken the bike.

3 An old comb from long ago is an _____ showing how people took care of their hair.

4 People who live in a cold, snowy _____ would want warm boots.

5 In the fall sky you can see the _____ of geese from north to south.

Word Study: The Suffix -al

The -al suffix means "relating to."

- If -al is added to a word that is a verb, the verb is changed to a noun.
- When the -al suffix is added to a noun, it changes the noun into an adjective.

> **arrive** (v.) to reach a place
> **arrival** (n.) the act of coming to a place
> **nation** (n.) a group of people that have the same laws and government
> **national** (adj.) something related to a nation

Add the -al suffix to each word. Use a dictionary to check your spelling.

		+ -al	Part of Speech
1	society		
2	environment		
3	culture		
4	region		

The Language of Testing

How would you answer a question like this on a test?

What factor was most important in the decision of some Indians to live near the ocean?

A. They liked the color blue.
B. They could find fish to eat.
C. They could go swimming.
D. They could bathe in the water.

 Tip

Another word for *factor* is *reason*.

Test Strategy: If the question says *what factor was most important*, ask yourself which reasons are not important. Cross off these wrong answers to help you find the correct answer. You might also rewrite the question using the word *reason* instead of factor.

1 How could you say the question above in a different way?

_____

_____

Try the strategy again by asking these questions in a different way.

2 What was the most important factor in helping Native Americans decide where to live?

A. finding dogs and cats
B. riding large horses
C. finding a safe place to build homes
D. finding bugs and frogs

_____

_____

_____

3 What was the most important factor in the migration of people from Asia to the Americas?

A. the cold weather in Asia
B. the wet weather in New York
C. the land bridge that joined Asia to America
D. the wild animals in Asia

_____

_____

_____

In Your Vocabulary Journal

Find each of these words in your American History Vocabulary Journal. Working by yourself or with a partner, use the definitions from pages 2 and 3 of your Work Text to complete the rest of the entry for each word.

artifact   civilization   contrast   culture   domesticate

environment   migration   region   society   speculate

7

Read the passage below. Think about the meanings of the new words printed in **bold**. Circle any familiar root words that might help you figure out what the new words mean. The first one has been done for you.

The Spanish in America

Vocabulary Strategy

Use words you know to help unlock the meaning of unfamiliar words. For example, *settle* can help you unlock the meaning of *settlement*, *settler*, and *unsettled*.

After Christopher Columbus explored America in 1492, the Spanish took over many parts of North and South America. They had two important (objectives), or goals. Their first objective was to find gold for Spain. The second was to **convert**, or change, the religious beliefs of the Native Americans.

The Spanish explorer, Francisco Pizarro, defeated South America's huge Inca **empire**. An empire is a group of nations that are ruled by a more powerful country. This Native American empire included parts of the nations we now call Peru, Ecuador, and Chile. At that time, there were no real **borders**, or separation lines, between these countries. After defeating the Incas, Pizarro sent huge amounts of Inca gold to Spain.

To convert the Native Americans, the Spanish built missions in the Southwest part of the United States. The missions had forts, churches, and farms and at least one **missionary**. The missionaries taught Native Americans about the Catholic religion.

New American History Words

border

noun   an imaginary line that divides states or countries

convert

verb   to change beliefs or to change form

noun   someone who has changed his or her beliefs

empire

noun   a group of nations that are ruled by a more powerful country

missionary

noun   a religious teacher

Now read this passage and practice the vocabulary strategy again. Circle familiar root words that are found in larger, unfamiliar words. Write the meaning of each circled root word near it.

The First English Settlement

In 1607, three English ships landed in Virginia with a **charter** from King James of England. The charter allowed the people on the ships to start a **settlement**. Soon after landing, the men built a fort, then a church, and then houses. To honor King James, the settlement was called Jamestown.

The English settlers hoped to find gold and become rich. However, they did not find gold during their first search. Other searches **confirmed** that there was no gold in Jamestown.

Native Americans who lived nearby taught the English to grow tobacco. The settlers learned that they could sell tobacco in England and earn a lot of money. So the Jamestown settlers began growing tobacco on large farms called **plantations**.

As time passed, the English and the Native Americans **exchanged** culture and information. From the Native Americans, the English learned to grow corn while Native Americans learned to grow onions from the English.

More New American History Words

charter

> *noun*   a document that allows a business, settlement, or government to exist

exchange

> *verb*   to swap or to trade
> *noun*   a swap or trade

plantation

> *noun*   a very large farm where crops are grown to be sold

settlement

> *noun*   a community built by people just moving into an area

Other Useful Words

confirm

> *verb*   to prove or show that information is true

objective

> *noun*   a purpose or goal
> *adjective*   fair and honest

My **objective** is to **exchange** these leaves for gold!

Apply the Strategy

Look at a chapter in your textbook that your teacher identifies. Look for words you know in larger, unfamiliar words to help you figure out the meaning of the new words. You can keep track of these word groups in a Word Web.

9

Finish the Sentence

Use a word from the box to finish each sentence. Write the correct word on the line. Discuss your choices with a partner.

convert	missionaries	border	empire	objectives

1. The Rio Grande forms the _____ separating the United States and Mexico.

2. Many Native Americans refused to _____, or change their beliefs.

3. One of Pizarro's _____ was to find gold for Spain.

4. Many mission schools were started by the _____.

5. The Spanish built an _____ in the Americas.

exchanged	plantations	charter	confirmed	settlement

6. The English settlers built a fort, church, and homes in a _____ they named Jamestown.

7. King James gave a group of people a _____, which gave them permission to start a settlement in North America.

8. A search of the area proved, or _____, that Native Americans had settled there first.

9. Native Americans _____, or traded, goods with the English settlers.

10. Cotton, tobacco, and sugar are grown on large farms called _____.

10

Would You Rather . . .

Take turns with a partner reading the questions below out loud. Think of a response and write it on the line. Write your responses in complete sentences. The first one has been done for you.

1 Would you rather live in a **settlement** or on a **plantation**? _I'd rather live in a_ _settlement because I would not like to be a farmer._

2 Would you rather build an **empire** or be a **missionary**? _____

_____

3 Would you rather **exchange** your apple for ice cream or **convert** it into apple sauce? _____

_____

4 Would you rather **confirm** the grade you made on your report or **speculate** about it? _____

_____

Quick Pick

Read each question either with a partner or by yourself. Think of a response and write it on the line. Explain your answer. The first one has been done for you.

1 Which could be a **border** between two countries: a river or a mud puddle?
A river, because it can separate two states or countries.

2 Would a **charter** give you permission to build a town or a house? _____

_____

3 If you were a **missionary**, would you teach baseball or religion? _____

_____

4 What would people build when they start a **settlement**: zoos or houses?

_____

The Right Word

Read each sentence. Look at the word or phrase that is underlined. Write a word from the box that means the same or almost the same thing as the underlined part of the sentence. Discuss your answers with a partner.

objective	border	convert	plantation	confirm

1 _____ On a <u>very large farm</u>, people grow crops that they can sell.

2 _____ The <u>goal or purpose</u> of basketball is to get the ball into the net.

3 _____ You can drive almost all day in Texas without going across the <u>line or marker between two states or countries</u> into another state.

4 _____ You should always <u>check or prove</u> that you have the right information on your ticket before getting on a plane.

5 _____ Some people choose to <u>change</u> to another religion for many different reasons.

Word Study: The Prefix *un-*

The prefix *un-* means *not*. When the *un-* prefix is added to the beginning of a word, it changes the meaning of the word to the opposite of what it meant before. The word becomes its own antonym!

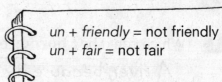

un + *friendly* = not friendly
un + *fair* = not fair

Complete the chart. Some of the spaces have been filled in for you. Use a dictionary to check your spellings and definitions.

		Part of Speech	+ *un-*	Definition
1	converted	adjective		has not changed one's beliefs
2	confirmed		unconfirmed	
3	settled	adjective		

The Language of Testing

How would you answer a question like this on a test?

What was **the main purpose of** the Spanish missions in California?

A. to start new farms
B. to explore the west coast
C. to convert the Native Americans to the Catholic religion
D. to teach reading to the Native Americans

Tip

The word *purpose* can mean *reason* or *use*. The word *main* shows you that you need to find the most important reason or use for something.

Test Strategy: If you see a question that uses the word *purpose*, rewrite it using the words *reason* or *use*. If the word *main* is in the question, make sure you choose the most important reason or use for something.

1 How could you say the question above in a different way?

_____

_____

Try the strategy again by asking these questions in a different way.

2 What was the main purpose of the Spanish conquest of the Inca Empire?

A. to teach the Incas to speak Spanish
B. to capture gold for Spain
C. to build a port on the Pacific Ocean
D. to bring horses to South America

_____

_____

_____

3 What was the main purpose of growing tobacco at Jamestown?

A. to sell the tobacco and earn a profit
B. to improve the soil near Jamestown
C. to become better farmers
D. to form friendships with Native Americans

_____

_____

_____

In Your Vocabulary Journal

Find each of these words in your American History Vocabulary Journal. Working by yourself or with a partner, use the definitions from pages 8 and 9 of your Work Text to complete the rest of the entry for each word.

border	charter	confirm	convert	empire
exchange	missionary	objective	plantation	settlement

Establishing the American Colonies

Read the passage below. Think about the meanings of the new words printed in **bold**. Underline any words or phrases that seem to be contrasted with the new words. Draw an arrow from each underlined word or phrase to the new word it is contrasted with. The first one has been done for you.

The Pilgrims Travel to America

Vocabulary Strategy

Use contrasts to help you understand the meanings of new words. Look for clues that point out contrasts such as *unlike*, *instead*, or *different from*.

In the early 1600s everyone in England was required to attend the Church of England. Unlike most people who followed this rule however, religious **dissenters** refused to attend the Church of England.

One group of dissenters decided to move to America to find religious freedom. They traveled on a small ship called the *Mayflower*. The people on the *Mayflower* were called the **Pilgrims**, because they were travelling in search of religious freedom. Ten of the people on the *Mayflower* were **indentured servants**. Unlike the people who paid to travel on the *Mayflower*, these indentured servants did not

pay. Instead, they would work as unpaid servants for a number of years in America.

Before leaving their ship, the Pilgrims wrote a **covenant**, or agreement, called the Mayflower Compact. This covenant said they would make laws that would be fair to all. The Pilgrims started a town called Plymouth in Massachusetts. They could not **predict** that in 1621 they would celebrate Thanksgiving with new Native American friends.

New American History Words

covenant

noun   a promise or a written agreement

dissenter

noun   a person who disagrees

indentured

adjective   describes a person who pays off a debt working for free

pilgrim

noun   a person who moves or travels to another place for religious reasons

Now read this passage and practice the vocabulary strategy again. Underline the words and phrases that use contrasts to show the meaning of **rebellion**.

More Colonies for England

In 1630, the Puritans left England for America because they wanted religious freedom. Their settlement grew into the Massachusetts **colony**, one of the thirteen English colonies.

The Puritans required everyone to pray in a Puritan church. A minister named Roger Williams believed that all people should be able to pray in their own way, however. The Puritans thought Roger Williams' ideas would not bring peace but could cause **rebellion**. They decided to send him back to England. However, Roger Williams escaped and started the Rhode Island colony of Providence.

William Penn also started a colony based on religious freedom. Penn belonged to the Quakers, a religious **sect**, or group, that disagreed with the Church of England. King Charles II of England made Penn the **proprietor**, or owner, of land that is now called Pennsylvania. The acceptance of all religions in Providence and Penn's colony **indicated** their leaders' belief in religious freedom.

More New American History Words

colony

noun   a settlement that belongs to another country

proprietor

noun   a person who owns land or a business

rebellion

noun   the act of fighting against the government or the people in charge

sect

noun   a group of people who have beliefs that are different from the main group

"Look! The **proprietor** put out a sign! Here's where we'll start our **colony**!"

Other Useful Words

indicate

verb   to show some kind of fact

predict

verb   to guess what might happen

Apply the Strategy

Look at a chapter in your textbook that your teacher identifies. Use contrasting words and phrases to help you figure out the meaning of any new words you find. Keep track of these contrasts in a chart.

Find the Word

Write a word from the box next to each clue. Then write the word formed by the boxed letters to answer the question below.

rebellion	indicate	dissenter	indentured	predict
pilgrim	sect	proprietor	colony	covenant

1 a person looking for religious freedom

2 someone who disagrees

3 a promise

4 to make a guess about something happening

5 owner of land or business

6 an action against a government

7 a group that has different beliefs

8 to show certain facts

9 a settlement ruled by another country

10 working without pay

What was William Penn called because he owned the land for the Pennsylvania colony?

A ___ ___ ___ ___ ___ ___ ___ ___ ___ ___ ___

16

Word Challenge: Correct or Incorrect?

Take turns with a partner reading the sentences below out loud. Write **C** if the sentence is correct, and write **I** if the sentence is incorrect. Rewrite the incorrect sentences. The first one has been done for you.

1 ___C___ A **covenant** is an agreement that must be kept.

2 _____ An **indentured** worker is paid well for his or her work.

_____

3 _____ Everyone lived peacefully during the **rebellion**.

_____

4 _____ The **colony** in Florida was ruled by Spain.

_____

Word Challenge: Finish the Idea

With a partner, take turns reading the incomplete sentences below. Write an ending for each. The first one has been done for you.

1 People might join a religious **sect** because _they dislike the ideas of_

the main religion.

2 A person would be called a **pilgrim** if _____

_____

3 A person might become a **dissenter** because _____

_____

4 A failing grade on a math test **indicates** _____

_____

17

Extend the Meaning

Write the letter of the word or phrase that best completes each sentence. Discuss your choices with a partner.

1 By signing a **covenant**, you would be making a _____.

   a. promise

   b. speech

   c. painting

2 A person might become an **indentured** servant if he or she _____.

   a. enjoyed cooking for others

   b. wanted to go to college

   c. could not afford to pay for the trip to America

3 People can try to **predict** _____.

   a. the winner of an election

   b. the number of pennies in a dollar

   c. the name of their school

4 Angry people might start a **rebellion** because _____.

   a. they want to change unfair laws

   b. they have enough food for their families

   c. they respect their king

Word Study: The Suffixes -er and -or

When the *-or* or *-er* suffix is added to a verb, two things happen.

- The verb is changed to a noun.
- The verb now refers to a person or tool that can do something.

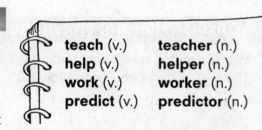

	teacher (n.)
teach (v.)	teacher (n.)
help (v.)	helper (n.)
work (v.)	worker (n.)
predict (v.)	predictor (n.)

Complete the chart. Use a dictionary to check your spelling and definitions.

		+ *-er* or *-or*	New Part of Speech	Definition
1	dissent			
2	indicate			
3	settle			
4	plant			

The Language of Testing

How would you answer a question like this on a test?

Based on the table and your knowledge of social studies, what colony was started in 1636?

A. Virginia   C. Rhode Island
B. Massachusetts   D. Pennsylvania

The phrase *based on the table and your knowledge of social studies* means you must read the chart and think about what you know about the topic.

The Founding of Four American Colonies

Date	Colony
1620	Pilgrims settled in Plymouth, Massachusetts
1630	Puritans started the Massachusetts Bay colony
1636	Roger Williams started the Rhode Island colony
1682	William Penn started the proprietary colony of Pennsylvania

Test Strategy:
- Always read the whole question and the answers first. Cross off the answers that you know are wrong. For example, there is no information in the chart about Virginia. Therefore, choice A must be wrong.
- Rewrite the question using the phrase *use the chart* instead of *based on the chart*.

Try the strategy again by asking these questions in a different way.

 1 Based on the chart and your knowledge of social studies, which people were the first to settle in New England?

A. Pilgrims   C. Puritans
B. Dutch   D. Spanish

_____

_____

 2 Based on the chart and your knowledge of social studies, which colony was started by a wealthy person?

A. Massachusetts   C. Pennsylvania
B. New York   D. Virginia

_____

_____

In Your Vocabulary Journal

Find each of these words in your American History Vocabulary Journal. Working by yourself or with a partner, use the definitions from pages 14 and 15 of your Work Text to complete the rest of the entry for each word.

colony	covenant	dissenter	indentured	indicate
pilgrim	predict	proprietor	rebellion	sect

Lesson 4

Economy and Trade in the Colonies

Read the passage below. Decide if each new word printed in **bold** is a noun, verb, or adjective and write it above each word. Then use that information with other clues in the text to figure what the new word means. The first one has been done for you.

Earning a Living in the Colonies

Vocabulary Strategy

Identify if a new word is used as a noun, verb, adjective, or adverb. This will help you use other clues in the text to figure out the meaning of the word.

noun

People earned a living in different ways throughout the thirteen American colonies. **Agriculture** was important but farmers grew different crops depending on the climate and soil. In the middle colonies, wheat was the **staple** crop. Rice and tobacco were staples in the southern colonies.

Agriculture was difficult in New England because of the region's long winters. Many people there fished and built ships. As the shipbuilding business **expanded**, ships built in New England sailed to Europe and Asia.

There were skilled people who worked in many crafts in the colonies, such as printmaking and candle making. These workers were called *masters*. They often hired teenaged boys to be their **apprentices**. An apprentice worked for his master for about seven years, learning skills. An apprentice's **duties** included cleaning the shop and making products. The apprentice system created many skilled crafts people in the thirteen colonies.

New American History Words

agriculture

   noun   farming and ranching

apprentice

   noun   a young person who works without pay to learn a job

duties

   noun   jobs and responsibilities, or taxes on goods brought into a country

staple

   noun   the main item grown or consumed in a region

   adjective   necessary, or main

Now read the passage below and practice the vocabulary strategy again. Write *noun, verb, or adjective* above each new word.

Mercantilism and Trade

The English wanted their thirteen American colonies to bring wealth to their nation. English ideas about wealth came from a theory called **mercantilism**. Mercantilism **emphasized** that a nation needed large amounts of gold and silver to be wealthy. England could earn gold and silver through new **enterprises**, such as trade with other nations. So England wanted to **export**, or sell to other nations, more goods than it **imported** from other nations. According to mercantilism, a nation had a strong balance of trade when it exported more than it imported. The nation earned gold by exporting goods.

England passed laws forcing American colonists to import certain goods only from England. The colonists were not allowed to export any products that they had made, however. The colonists imported more than they exported so they did not have a good balance of trade. As time passed, the colonists grew angry with England's unfair laws.

More New American History Words

enterprise
noun   a business undertaking or new project

export
verb   to sell goods to another country
noun   an item sold to another country

import
verb   to buy products from other countries
noun   an item bought from another country

mercantilism
noun   a theory that a nation must sell more products than it buys to be wealthy and strong

Other Useful Words

emphasize
verb   to show that something is very important

expand
verb   to make something larger

"I think I need a new **enterprise**."

Apply the Strategy

Look at a chapter in your textbook that your teacher identifies. Identify the parts of speech of new words to help you figure out their meanings.

Finish the Paragraphs

Use the words in bold to finish the paragraphs below. Write the correct words in the blanks. One word from each box will not be used.

agriculture	expanded	staple	apprentice	duties

Most people in the thirteen colonies worked in _____ to raise crops **(1)**

and animals. Wheat was the most important, or _____ crop in the **(2)**

middle colonies. Many people also worked at such jobs as printmaking or shoemaking. A boy

could learn one of these trades by becoming an _____ and working for **(3)**

a master craftsman for a number of years. Cleaning the shop and making new products were

some of an apprentice's _____. **(4)**

export	colony	emphasized	mercantilism	import

According to the ideas of _____, a nation needed to earn gold **(5)**

through trade with other countries. So England passed laws that _____ **(6)**

the importance of controlling trade with the colonies. These laws required the colonies to buy,

or _____, their manufactured goods from England. The colonies were **(7)**

required to _____ most raw materials like wood and cotton to England. **(8)**

Word Challenge: Word Association

Take turns with a partner reading the groups of words below. Write the word from the lesson that best goes with each group. The first one has been done for you.

1 _agriculture_ farming, crops

2 _____ increase, grow, add detail

3 _____ imports, taxes, money

4 _____ to stress, to insist

5 _____ business, new project

Word Challenge: Example/Not an Example

With a partner or by yourself, think of things that are and are not examples of the words listed below. Write your responses in the chart. The first one has been done for you.

		Example	Not an Example
1	apprentice	You work with a shoemaker to learn skills, but you don't get paid.	You work at a store and get paid every week.
2	mercantilism		
3	staple		
4	colony		

Analogies

Use a word from the box to finish each sentence. Write the word on the line. Discuss your answers with a partner.

export	agriculture	expand	apprentice

1 Student is to teacher as _____ is to master.

2 Reduce is to shrink as increase is to _____.

3 Fishing is to sea as _____ is to land.

4 Arrive is to leave as import is to _____.

Word Study: The Root *port*

port (v.) to carry

Port is the root in the words *import* and *export*. The root word *port* means "to carry." When a prefix or a suffix is added to *port,* a new word is formed.

A. Circle the root word in each larger word and write a definition for each. Use a dictionary to check your definitions.

		Definition
1	**transportation**	
2	**portable**	
3	**porter**	

B. Use a word from the chart to finish each sentence.

1 This summer, I worked as a _____. I carried people's suitcases.

2 Airplanes and trains are two kinds of _____.

3 My laptop computer is easy to carry. It is very _____.

24

The Language of Testing

How would you answer a question like this on a test?

"An apprentice should never complain. He has a place to live, food to eat, and a master to work with."

What does this statement illustrate?

A. Every apprentice works very hard.
B. It is good to be an apprentice.
C. Craftsmen do not treat apprentices well.
D. An apprentice works too many years.

 Tip

The phrase *what does this statement illustrate* means that you need to read the statement and decide what it means. Then choose the answer that is closest in meaning to the statement.

Test Strategy: If the question has the phrase *what does this statement illustrate*, restate the question to ask *what does this statement mean?* The answer you choose should be closest in meaning to the statement.

Try the strategy again with these questions. Cross out *illustrate* and write *mean*. Then cross out the answer choices that do not mean the same as the statement.

1 "It is unfair that the colonies must buy most manufactured goods from England."

What does this statement illustrate?

A. The colonies did not agree with the English trade laws.
B. The colonies did not want to produce their own goods.
C. The colonies have too much trade with each other.
D. England does not produce enough goods for the colonies.

2 "England can become a rich nation through lots of exports and a favorable balance of trade."

What does this statement illustrate?

A. England imports too many products.
B. England agrees with the mercantilism theory.
C. England should import its manufacured goods.
D. England is a poor nation.

In Your Vocabulary Journal

Find each of these words in your American History Vocabulary Journal. Working by yourself or with a partner, use the definitions from pages 21 and 22 of your Work Text to complete the rest of the entry for each word.

agriculture	apprentice	duties	emphasize	enterprise
expand	export	import	mercantilism	staple

Lesson 5 Conflict in the Colonies

Read the passage below. Think about the meanings of the words printed in **bold**. Create associations between words you know and the new words. These will help you remember what the new words mean. Mark these associations in the passage. The first one has been done for you.

The Colonists Against the British

Vocabulary Strategy

Create associations between things you know and the new words to "anchor" your understanding of the new words. You can complete a word anchor chart to help you create associations.

In Britain, or England, people chose the members of Parliament. Parliament is where British laws are made. American colonists also chose people to write laws in their own **assemblies** that were somewhat like Parliament.

Parliament wrote laws that required American colonists to pay more **tariffs**. These tariffs taxed imported goods like sugar, tea, and paper. The colonists **debated** these tariffs. Some argued that the tariff laws were not fair because they had not chosen the members of Parliament. Some also began to **boycott** British goods. They stopped buying British cloth and made their own cloth instead.

Problems with Britain grew worse. On March 5, 1770, there was a fight in Boston, Massachusetts between British soldiers and colonists. Three colonists were killed. The event became known as the Boston Massacre. It was used as **propaganda** to turn colonists against the British. It seemed to work.

New American History Words

assembly

noun a group of individuals who are chosen by the people to make laws

boycott

verb to refuse to buy certain goods or services

noun the act of refusing to buy certain goods or services

propaganda

noun ideas spread to change people's opinions about someone or something

tariff

noun a tax on goods that are imported from another country

Now read this passage and practice the vocabulary strategy again. Write near the new words or mark in the text any associations that will help you "anchor" the meaning of the new words.

The Colonists Prepare to Fight

After the Boston Massacre, colonists **organized** protests against the British. Citizens also formed **militias**. These citizen armies called themselves Minutemen. They needed only a minute to be ready to fight.

The British **repealed**, or ended, some laws such as the Stamp Act. But Americans still had to pay a tax on tea. **Sedition** grew stronger. Angry Americans **organized** the Boston Tea Party. On December 16, 1773, a group of colonists dressed as Native Americans. They went aboard the tea ships in Boston Harbor and dumped tea in the harbor. They dumped so much tea into the harbor that the water turned brown!

King George wrote laws to punish the colonists. His laws showed **intolerance** for their feelings. He didn't care that they wanted different laws. The colonists hated the new laws so much they called them the Intolerable Acts. Many colonists believed that they would have to fight for the freedom they wanted.

More New American History Words

intolerance

noun   disrespect for others and their beliefs

militia

noun   an army made up of citizens, not soldiers

repeal

verb   to end or remove a law

sedition

noun   attempts to stir up anger against the government

"If we want this **propaganda** to work, we need to make King George more **intolerable**!"

Other Useful Words

debate

verb   to discuss a topic from different points of view

noun   a discussion in which people argue different points of view

organize

verb   to put into order

Apply the Strategy

Look at a chapter in your textbook that your teacher identifies. Use associations to help you anchor your understanding of any new words you find.

The Right Word

Read each sentence. Look at the word or phrase that is underlined. Write a word from the box that means the same or almost the same thing as the underlined part of the sentence. Discuss your answers with a partner.

debate	tariff	assembly	boycotted

1. _____ Our state has an elected <u>group of lawmakers who write new laws</u>.

2. _____ The <u>tax</u> on cars from other countries made the cars more expensive.

3. _____ We <u>refused to buy</u> that company's products because they were not safe.

4. _____ Pedro and Ali like to <u>discuss issues from different points of view</u>.

repeal	intolerance	militia	organize

5. _____ My mother said we must <u>put everything in order in</u> our rooms before we can go to the mall.

6. _____ Marie showed <u>she could not respect or accept the ideas and opinions of other people</u>.

7. _____ The Americans wanted Parliament to <u>end</u> unfair tariff laws.

8. _____ The people formed a <u>citizen army</u> to fight the British.

Word Challenge: Finish the idea

With a partner, take turns reading the incomplete sentences below. Write an ending for each. The first one has been done for you.

1 It is wrong to show **intolerance** to others because ___we should show respect for___ ___everyone's beliefs.___

2 I should **organize** my desk because _____

_____

3 The candidates for president always **debate** the issues because _____

_____

4 Harmful laws should be **repealed** because _____

_____

Word Challenge: What's Your Answer?

Take turns with a partner reading each question out loud and writing the answer on the line. Answer the questions with complete sentences. The first one has been done for you.

1 What kind of work would be done in an **assembly**? ___The people who___

___are chosen to work there make laws.___

2 What kind of statements would show **sedition** against a government? _____

_____

3 What are some reasons why you might join a **boycott**? _____

_____

4 What kind of **propaganda** could be dangerous? _____

_____

Synonyms or Antonyms

Look at each group of words below. Circle the two words in each group that are synonyms or the two words that are antonyms. Write synonyms or antonyms on the line. Discuss your choices with a partner.

1
  boycott   staple

  charter   buy

_____

3
  tariff   tax

  organize   sedition

_____

2
  intolerance   disapproval

  debate   assembly

_____

4
  assembly   lawmakers

  militia   dissenter

_____

Word Study: The Prefixes *in-* and *im-*

The prefixes *in-* and *im-* mean *not*. Consequently, when you add one of them to a noun like *tolerance*, the word means the opposite of what it did before.

tolerance (n.) respecting the ideas and beliefs of others
intolerance (n.) not accepting or respecting ideas that are different

A. Add *in-* or *im-* to the words below and write a definintion. Use a dictionary to check your spelling and definitions.

		+ *im-* or *in-*	Definition
1	possible		
2	experienced		
3	convenient		
4	direct		

B. Replace the underlined words with a word from the chart.

1 It was <u>not possible</u> for us to finish our homework tonight. _____

2 It was <u>not easy</u> to pick up Sumaya at the airport. _____

The Language of Testing

How would you answer a question like this on a test?

All of the following are true

except

   A. The English ruled thirteen American colonies.
   B. Every colony had its own lawmaking group.
   C. The colonies traded with England.
   D. The colonists were happy to pay tariffs on tea and sugar.

💡 **Tip**

The word *except* means you should look for something that is opposite of the word or phrase before *except*. In this question you need to look for the answer that is false.

Test Strategy: If you see a question that has the word *except* in it, ask the question in a different way. Remember that you are looking for the answer that is false.

1 How could you say the question above in a different way?

_____

_____

Try the strategy again by asking these questions in a different way.

2 All of the following are true except

   A. Virginia's assembly was called the House of Burgesses.
   B. Every colony voted for lawmakers.
   C. Americans voted for people to represent them in Parliament.
   D. Parliament made English laws.

3 The colonists protested against Britain in all of the following ways except

   A. The colonies formed militias.
   B. Americans bought British goods.
   C. Americans started a boycott against British goods.
   D. During the Boston Tea Party, tea was dumped into Boston Harbor.

_____

_____

_____

_____

_____

_____

In Your Vocabulary Journal

Find each of these words in your American History Vocabulary Journal. Working by yourself or with a partner, use the definitions from pages 26 and 27 of your Work Text to complete the rest of the entry for each word.

assembly	**boycott**	**debate**	**intolerance**	**militia**
organize	**propaganda**	**repeal**	**sedition**	**tariff**

Lesson 6

The American Revolution

Read the passage below. Underline the words in **bold** print that have more than one meaning. You may check the definitions below for help. The first one has been done for you.

The Colonists Choose War

Vocabulary Strategy

Identify words in the passage that have more than one, or multiple, meanings. In some cases a word can be used as different parts of speech. Understanding multiple meanings will help you create a fuller understanding of new words.

In 1774 leaders from the colonies met at the First Continental **Congress** in Philadelphia to solve their problems with King George. The leaders wrote a **petition** in which they **proposed** that the king change unfair laws. But King George ignored the petition when he received it.

In 1775 colonial leaders met at the Second Continental Congress in Philadelphia and sent another petition to King George. But King George refused to even read their petition! So the Congress decided that the colonies should become a free and independent nation.

One of the youngest men at the Congress, Thomas Jefferson,

agreed to write a document that explained why the colonists wanted **independence** from Britain. This document was called the Declaration of Independence. Congress approved the Declaration of Independence on July 4, 1776.

The colonists fought the British army to win their independence. This war was a **revolution** because it completely changed their government. This war later came to be called the American Revolution.

New American History Words

congress

noun   a large meeting held to make decisions about laws and government, or the lawmaking branch of the United States government

independence

noun   the state of being free from outside control

petition

noun   a written request

verb   to make a request

revolution

noun   a change in government that involves war, or a major change in the way people live

Now read the passage below and practice the vocabulary strategy again. Check the definitions on this page for words with multiple meanings. Underline the words in **bold** print that have more than one meaning.

The Fight for Freedom

During the American Revolution many people were **patriots** who loved their country and fought for independence from British control. Unlike the patriots, many people in the colonies were loyal to Britain. These people were called **Loyalists**. They helped the British during the war. Another group that fought was the **mercenary** soldiers. These were German soldiers who were paid by the British to fight the colonists.

The leader of the colonial army was General George Washington. Many paintings **portray** Washington as unsmiling and unfriendly. However, Washington cared about his soldiers. He also refused to give up although he lost many battles.

Washington and his army defeated the powerful British army in 1781. In 1783 British leaders signed a peace **treaty** with the new nation. That new nation was called the United States of America.

More New American History Words

loyalist

noun   a person who remains loyal to a government, or someone who was loyal to Great Britain during the American Revolution

mercenary

noun   a soldier who fights for pay

adjective   doing something just for pay or personal gain

patriot

noun   a person who loves his or her country, or an American colonist who fought for independence

treaty

noun   an agreement between two or more nations

Other Useful Words

portray

verb   to show a person, thing, or event in a certain way

propose

verb   to suggest a plan

Apply the Strategy

Look at a chapter in your textbook that your teacher identifies. Find out if any of the new words you find have multiple meanings. Keep track of these multiple meanings in a chart.

Matching

Finish the sentences in Group A with words from Group B. Write the letter of the word on the line. Discuss your choices with a partner.

Group A

1 Leaders of the Continental Congress suggested, or _____ that a petition be sent to King George.

2 The colonists decided they wanted to be free from British control, so they declared _____.

3 People who love and support their country are called _____.

4 Colonists who felt loyal to Britain were called _____.

Group B

A. patriots
B. proposed
C. Loyalists
D. independence

Group A

5 The colonists fought a _____ to win their freedom from Britain.

6 The British paid _____ soldiers to fight against Americans.

7 Members of the Continental Congress sent a _____ to King George asking him to change the laws.

8 After Americans defeated the British, the United States and Britain agreed to peace by signing a _____.

Group B

E. mercenary
F. treaty
G. revolution
H. petition

Word Challenge: Would You Rather . . .

Take turns with a partner reading the questions below out loud. Think of a response and write it on the line. Write your responses in complete sentences. The first one has been done for you.

1. Would you rather have been a **mercenary** or a **patriot** in the American Revolution? _I would have rather been a patriot so that I would have believed in what I was fighting for._

2. Would you rather show your **independence** or be a **loyalist**? _____

_____

3. Would you rather fight a **revolution** or a sign a **petition** to change a situation? _____

_____

4. Would you rather **propose** a **treaty** with your enemies or **petition** them to change? _____

_____

Word Challenge: Quick Pick

Read each question with a partner or by yourself. Think of a response and write it on the line. Explain your answer. The first one has been done for you.

1. What could be planned at a **congress**: new laws or a new playground?
   Congress would plan new laws.

2. What would a **loyalist** do: support or fight against the government? _____
   _____

3. How would you **portray** your family to your friends: would you describe
   them or would you refuse to talk about them? _____
   _____

4. What should a teacher **propose** to a class: a new video game or a new
   project? _____
   _____

Finish the Idea

Finish each idea to make a complete sentence. Write your answer on the line. Discuss your answers with a partner.

1 I would call someone a **patriot** if he or she _____

_____

2 You could call someone **mercenary** if _____

_____

3 I would call a change in society a **revolution** if _____

_____

4 If I was an artist, I would **portray** my best friend as _____

_____

Word Study: The Suffix -tion

When you add the suffix -tion to a verb such as *decorate*, two things happen.
- The verb changes to a noun: *decoration*.
- The word now refers to an item that you add to something to make it more attractive.

decorate (v.) to make something more attractive
decoration (n.) something you add to something else to make it more attractive

A. Add the -tion suffix to the following words and write your own definition. Use a dictionary to check your spelling and your definitions.

	+ -tion	Definition
1 locate		
2 propose		
3 revolt		

B. Use a word from the chart with the -tion suffix to finish each sentence.

1 The beach is a good place, or _____ for a summer party.

2 The community liked Anya's suggestion, or _____ that the city build a new skate park.

The Language of Testing

How would you answer a question like this on a test?

What was the result of the First
Continental Congress?

   A. The British changed all unfair laws.
   B. The colonists ended their boycott.
   C. Most Americans became Loyalists.
   D. Americans sent a petition to King George.

Tip

The phrase *what was the result of* can also mean *what happened after.*

Test Strategy: When you find a question that asks you for the result of something, you are supposed to look for a cause and effect relationship. You can rewrite the question using *what happened because of* or *what happened after* instead of *what was the result of.*

1 How could you say the question above in a different way?

_____

_____

Try the strategy again by asking these questions in a different way.

2 One result of the Boston Tea Party was

   A. the Boston Massacre
   B. more trade between the colonies and Britain
   C. an increase in colonists drinking more tea
   D. King George's punishment of the colonists in Boston

3 What was one result of the American Revolution?

   A. The British sent petitions to the United States.
   B. King George became popular in the United States.
   C. The colonies became independent.
   D. Colonists began to travel to Britain.

_____

_____

_____

In Your Vocabulary Journal

Find each of these words in your American History Vocabulary Journal. Working by yourself or with a partner, use the definitions from pages 32 and 33 of your Work Text to complete the rest of the entry for each word.

congress	**independence**	**loyalist**	**mercenary**	**patriot**
petition	**portray**	**propose**	**revolution**	**treaty**

The Constitution and the Bill of Rights

Read the passage below. Think about the meaning of the words printed in **bold**. Circle any words that end with -cy, -ic, and -ism. Write what each suffix means near it in the passage. Remember that -cy names a type of government, -ic describes a connection, and -ism names a belief. The first one has been done for you.

type of government

Planning the Constitution

Vocabulary Strategy

Identify suffixes that can help you understand the meaning of new words.

American leaders wanted their country to be a (**democracy**) in which the American people would govern themselves. In 1787 they wrote laws called the United States Constitution in order to do just that.

The Constitution has **sovereignty** over all other laws. This means the Constitution is the highest law in the nation.

One goal of the Constitution was to create a **republic**. We can **define** republic as a government without a king or queen in which citizens elect their leaders. A second goal was to create a government based on the ideas of **federalism**. Federalism is defined as a system in which powers are shared by the federal, or national, government and the state governments.

A third goal was that new laws called **amendments** could be added to the Constitution when needed. Since 1787, twenty seven amendments have been added.

New American History Words

amendment

noun   a law that is added to the Constitution, or a change that is made to make a law or rule better

democracy

noun   a system of government in which people choose their leaders and laws

federalism

noun   sharing of powers between the state government and the national government

republic

noun   a country in which citizens vote for government leaders

sovereignty

noun   a nation's power to control its own government

Now read this passage and circle any words that end with *-ive* and *-al*. Write what each suffix means near it in the passage. Remember that *-ive* describes a characteristic, and *-al* describes a connection to an idea.

The Three Branches of Government

The writers of the Constitution divided the government powers into three branches. The first branch is the legislative or lawmaking branch. Lawmakers work in the two houses of Congress — the Senate and the House of Representatives. Members of Congress **legislate** new laws for the nation. Americans elect **representatives** to legislate for them in Congress.

The second branch is the **executive** branch. Its job is to carry out the laws made by Congress. The President leads the executive branch.

The **judicial** branch is the third branch. The judicial branch controls the nation's court system. The United States Supreme Court is the highest court in the judicial branch.

In 1787, the writers of the Constitution had **omitted** laws to protect personal freedom, however. The Bill of Rights was added to the Constitution in 1791. It contains ten amendments that protect the rights of every American.

More New American History Words

executive

adjective   having to do with putting laws into action

judicial

adjective   having to do with the courts and judges

legislate

verb   to make and pass laws

representative

noun   a person who is elected to make laws in Congress, or a person who acts for other people

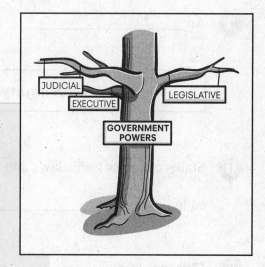

JUDICIAL
EXECUTIVE
LEGISLATIVE
GOVERNMENT POWERS

Other Useful Words

define

verb   to explain what something means

omit

verb   to leave out or not include

Apply the Strategy

Look at a chapter in your textbook that your teacher identifies. Use familiar prefixes and suffixes to help you figure out the meaning of any new words you find.

Finish the Sentence

Use a word from the box to finish each sentence. Write the correct word on the line. Discuss your choices with a partner.

legislate	republic	amendment	executive	judicial

1 The _____ branch carries out the nation's laws.

2 Members of the House of Representatives and Senate _____ new laws.

3 Judges work in the courts as part of the _____ branch.

4 The United States is a _____ because citizens elect leaders.

5 An _____ is a law that has been added to the Constitution.

omit	sovereignty	representatives	federalism	define

6 States can pass traffic laws and the federal government can print money under the system called _____.

7 Citizens elect _____ who will represent them in Congress.

8 The Constitution has _____ over all other laws of the United States.

9 We can _____ constitution as a set of laws that govern a nation.

10 It is a mistake to _____ the sugar when baking a cake.

40

Word Challenge: Definitions

Take turns with a partner reading the questions out loud. Draw a line through each incorrect definition. Then rewrite each incorrect definition. If a definition is correct, write a sentence using the new word. The first one has been done for you.

1 A **republic** is a nation without a king or queen. _Yes. A republic is a nation that_ _has a prime minister or president as its leader._

2 **Omit** means to leave something out. _____

_____

3 **Federalism** means that state and federal governments share power. _____

_____

4 **Sovereignty** means that a nation can be a colony of another country. _____

_____

Word Challenge: What's Your Answer?

Take turns with a partner reading each question out loud and writing an answer on the line. Answer the questions with complete sentences. The first one has been done for you.

1 Why would the Constitution need an **amendment**? _Certain rights_ _were left out of the original Constitution._

2 What would a person do as a **representative** in Congress? _____

_____

3 What do you do when you **define** words? _____

_____

4 What would you do if you worked in the **executive** branch? _____

_____

Analogies

Use a word from the box to finish each sentence. Write the word on the line. Discuss your answers with a partner.

legislate	omit	judicial	define

1 Execute is to carry out laws as _____ is to pass laws.

2 Include is to take in as _____ is to leave out.

3 Build is to toolbox as _____ is to dictionary.

4 Executive branch is to President as _____ branch is to Chief Justice.

Word Study: The Suffix -ism

When you add the suffix -ism to an adjective like regional, it does two things.

- It changes the adjective to a noun: regionalism.
- It changes the meaning of the word. The word now refers to something that belongs to a certain region.

regional (adj.) having to do with a certain area
regionalism (n.) something that belongs to a certain region

A. Complete the chart. Use a dictionary to check your spelling and definitions.

	+ -ism	Definition
1 federal		
2 colonial		
3 agricultural		
4 loyal		

B. Use a word from the chart to finish each sentence.

1 The soldier who fought on the side of the government showed _____.

2 A country that wants to build colonies is interested in _____.

The Language of Testing

How would you answer a question like this on a test?

Identify the branch of government that contains two houses of Congress.

    A. judicial branch
    B. executive branch
    C. legislative branch
    D. colonial branch

 Tip

The word *identify* means *to point out* or *name*. In a test question, it means that you need to choose or pick the correct answer.

Test Strategy: If you see a question that uses the word *identify*, rewrite it using the words *pick* or *choose*.

1 How could you say the question above in a different way?

_____

_____

Try the strategy again by asking these questions in a different way.

2 Which of these was not a goal when the Constitution was written?

    A. to protect the sovereignty of the United States
    B. to create a republic
    C. to create a Parliament
    D. to create three branches of government

3 Which of these people is part of the executive branch?

    A. senators
    B. judges
    C. the President
    D. representatives

_____   _____

_____   _____

_____   _____

In Your Vocabulary Journal

Find each of these words in your American History Vocabulary Journal. Working by yourself or with a partner, use the definitions from pages 38 and 39 of your Work Text to complete the rest of the entry for each word.

amendment   **define**   **democracy**   **executive**   **federalism**   **judicial**

legislate   **omit**   **representative**   **republic**   **sovereignty**

Lesson 8

Growth of the New Nation

Read the first passage below. Think about the meaning of the new words printed in **bold**. Underline any definitions in the text that might help you figure out what the new words mean. The first one has been done for you.

The United States Expands

Vocabulary Strategy

Look for definitions in the text to help you understand the meanings of new words.

After the American Revolution, the United States ruled thirteen states along the Atlantic Ocean and all of the land to the east of the Mississippi River. <u>The unsettled land between the states and the Mississippi River was called the</u> **frontier**. Soon after the American Revolution ended, many Americans began to settle the frontier. They were called **pioneers** because they were the first to move out of the colonies and into new lands. They cleared forests and built farms and cabins.

American **expansion**, or growth, angered the Native Americans who lived on the frontier. They feared that the pioneers would take away their land.

In 1830, Congress passed a law called the Indian **Removal** Act, which forced Native Americans who lived east of the Mississippi River to move to land that was west of the river. The removal of 100,000 Native Americans during the 1830s and 1840s has been **described** as unfair and cruel.

New American History Words

expansion
  noun   the act of growing larger

frontier
  noun   the outer edge of settled land

pioneer
  noun   one of the first people of a group to settle in an area, or to do something
  verb   to be one of the first people to do something

removal
  noun   the act of taking or moving away

Now read the passage below and practice the strategy again. Underline any definitions in the passage that can help you figure out what the new words in **bold** mean.

A Changing Nation

After the United States bought the Louisiana Purchase from France in 1803 it owned a huge **territory**, or land, that was west of the Mississippi River. President Thomas Jefferson wanted information about the Louisiana territory so he sent an **expedition**, or group of explorers, to explore it. Meriwether Lewis and William Clark led the expedition of about forty men across the territory. As they traveled, Lewis and Clark kept journals and **illustrated** them with pictures of the plants and animals they found.

In 1823, President James Monroe wrote a document called the Monroe Doctrine. This doctrine, a document which explained his ideas, stated that Europeans could never rule colonies in America again. The United States would stay out of Europe's problems as well.

Americans in different states wanted easier ways to trade with each other. So they built **canals**, or artificial waterways, for shipping goods from one place to another. The famous Erie Canal helped New York City become the nation's busiest port.

More New American History Words

canal
  noun   an artificial waterway

expedition
  noun   a group that makes a trip for a specific reason, or a journey of exploration

territory
  noun   land that a nation controls

A **pioneer**'s work is never done!

Other Useful Words

describe
  verb   to tell what something is like

illustrate
  verb   to draw pictures for a book, to explain, or to show

Apply the Strategy

Look at a chapter in your textbook that your teacher identifies. Use definitions in the text to help you figure out the meaning of any new words you find.

Find the Word

Write a word from the box next to each clue. Then write the word made by the boxed letters to answer the question below. One word will be used twice.

pioneer	**expedition**	**canal**	**illustrate**	**frontier**
describe	**removal**	**territory**	**expansion**	

1 to draw a picture of something _____ _____ _____ _____ _____ _____ ☐

2 a journey of exploration _____ ☐ _____ _____ _____ _____ _____ _____

3 growth _____ _____ _____ ☐ _____ _____ _____ _____

4 taking away _____ _____ ☐ _____ _____ _____

5 to tell what something is like ☐ _____ _____ _____ _____ _____ _____

6 show or explain ☐ _____ _____ _____ _____ _____ _____

7 land controlled by a nation ☐ _____ _____ _____ _____ _____ _____

8 the first to settle an area _____ ☐ _____ _____ _____ _____ _____

9 unsettled land _____ _____ ☐ _____ _____ _____ _____

10 waterway _____ _____ ☐ _____ _____

What did Lewis and Clark lead? An _____ _____ _____ _____ _____ _____ _____ _____ _____

Word Challenge: Word Association

Take turns with a partner reading the groups of words below out loud. Write the word from the lesson that goes best with each group. The first one has been done for you.

1 _____**pioneers**_____ new settlers, lead the way

2 _____ team, journey, voyage

3 _____ land, country, control

4 _____ growing larger, spreading out

5 _____ draw pictures, explain

Word Challenge: Would You Rather . . .

Take turns with a partner reading the questions below out loud. Think of a response and write it on the line. Explain your answers. The first one has been done for you.

1 Would your rather help with garbage **removal** or garbage **expansion**? _I'd rather_

help with the garbage removal because there's already too much garbage.

2 Would you rather **describe** your favorite car in a paragraph or **illustrate** it? _____

_____

3 Would you rather be a **pioneer** or be part of an **expedition**? _____

_____

4 Would you rather live on the **frontier** or in a **territory**? _____

_____

47

Extend the Meaning

Write the letter of the word or phrase that best completes each sentence. Discuss your choices with a partner.

1 To **describe** a painting, you would talk about _____.

    a. colonies and settlements

    b. Native American clothing

    c. colors, shapes, and pictures

2 You might want to **illustrate** _____.

    a. a road map

    b. a story book

    c. a charter

3 You might wish to join an **expedition** to _____.

    a. swim in a hotel pool

    b. climb a very tall mountain

    c. read a library book

4 **Expansion** of the United States was helped by the _____.

    a. writing of the Constitution

    b. mercenary soldiers

    c. Louisiana Purchase

Word Study: The Root *mov*

Mov is the root in the words *movie* and *removal*. The root *mov* means *move*.

You can make many *mov* words by adding:
- prefixes like *re-*, *un-*, and *im-*
- suffixes like *-ment*, *-able*, and *-ability*

Add the prefixes and suffixes below to the root *mov* to make new words. Write a definition for each new word. Use a dictionary to check your spelling and definitions.

	Prefixes	Suffixes	Word	Definition
1	re-		remove	
2	re-	-able		
3		-ment		
4	im-	-able		

The Language of Testing

How would you answer a question like this on a test?

The Lewis and Clark expedition

was characterized by _____.

    A. pioneers settling on the frontier
    B. the building of the Erie Canal
    C. men exploring the Louisiana territory
    D. new tariffs on American goods

Tip

The phrase *was characterized by* means you must find one answer that has information about the topic of the question.

Test Strategy: Look for an answer that has the best information for the question.

1 How could you ask the question above in a different way?

_____

_____

Try the strategy again by asking these questions in a different way.

2 The Monroe Doctrine was characterized by _____.

    A. words from the Bill of Rights
    B. explanation that European countries should stay out of America
    C. its warning to King George
    D. a plan to explore new territories

3 The Indian Removal Act was characterized by _____.

    A. the forced movement of Native Americans to land west of the Mississippi
    B. new leadership
    C. a battle to win land in Florida
    D. the movement of people to Canada

_____   _____

_____   _____

_____   _____

In Your Vocabulary Journal

Find each of these words in your American History Vocabulary Journal. Working by yourself or with a partner, use the definitions from pages 44 and 45 of your Work Text to complete the rest of the entry for each word.

canal	**describe**	**expansion**	**expedition**	**frontier**
illustrate	**pioneer**	**removal**	**territory**	

The Civil War and Reconstruction

Read the passage below. Think about the meaning of the new words printed in **bold**. Circle familiar words in some of the new words that might help you figure out their meaning. The first one has been done for you.

The United States is Divided

Vocabulary Strategy

Use words you know to help unlock the meaning of unfamiliar words in the same family. For example, *construct* can help you unlock the meaning of *reconstruct* and *reconstruction*.

Slaves were first brought from Africa to work in the American colonies in the 1600s. In the South, people depended on (slavery) to run their huge cotton, sugar, and tobacco plantations. But many people in the North thought slavery was wrong. They wanted to abolish, or end, slavery. Anger about the **abolition** of slavery grew between the North and South.

In 1861, Abraham Lincoln was elected President. The South believed Lincoln would end slavery. As a result, eleven Southern states decided to **secede**, or stop being part of the United States. They formed their own country called the Confederate States of America, or the **Confederacy**. Some of the states in the Confederacy were Texas, Virginia, Georgia, and Florida. Their names can be **abbreviated** as TX, VA, GA, and FL.

In 1861, the United States and the Confederacy began to fight. This war is called the Civil War. Thousands of Americans were killed during the four years of this terrible war.

New American History Words

abolition

noun the act of ending something, especially slavery

confederacy

noun a group of states or people with the same goals, or the group of states that broke away from the United States in 1860–1861

secede

verb to leave a group

slavery

noun the practice of owning people as property

Now read the passage below and practice the vocabulary strategy again. Underline familiar words that are found in larger, unfamiliar words.

After the Civil War

President Lincoln issued the **Emancipation** Proclamation in 1863. This document said slaves in the Confederacy were free. However, slaves really received emancipation, or freedom, after the Civil War ended in 1865. In that year the Thirteenth Amendment ended slavery forever.

After the Confederacy surrendered, the North and South were one nation again. Much of the South had to be rebuilt after the war, however. The years after the Civil War were called **Reconstruction**. This name refers to the rebuilding of the South.

The events of Reconstruction can be **summarized**, or stated briefly, in a few sentences. Soldiers were sent to control the South. Cities, railroads, and farms were rebuilt. In 1872, Congress gave **amnesty**, or the government's forgiveness, to most people in the South.

The North and the South **compromised** about when the army should leave the South. The Compromise of 1877 said the army would leave and the southern states would rejoin the United States. In return, African Americans in the South would be allowed to vote.

More New American History Words

amnesty

noun   government forgiveness of crimes

compromise

verb   to give up something to end an argument

noun   an agreement reached when both sides give up something they want to solve an argument

emancipation

noun   freedom from something, especially slavery

reconstruction

noun   a period of rebuilding, or the rebuilding of the South after the Civil War

Other Useful Words

abbreviate

verb   to shorten

summarize

verb   to explain briefly by telling the most important ideas

Please **summarize** your feelings about the **Confederacy**, Mr. President.

We will never **compromise** and accept the Confederacy.

Apply the Strategy

Look at a chapter in your textbook that your teacher identifies. Use familiar words to help you unlock the meaning of unfamiliar words.

Finish the Paragraphs

Use the words in bold to finish each paragraph below. Write the words in the blanks. One word in each box will not be used. Discuss your choices with a partner.

slavery	staple	Confederacy	seceded	abolition

Many people in the North thought _____ was wrong. Therefore,
1

they worked for the _____ of slavery. In the South, people believed they
2

needed slaves for their plantations. In 1861, eleven southern states left the United States when

they _____. They started a country called the Confederate States of
3

America. The abbreviated name was the _____.
4

amnesty	revolution	emancipation	Reconstruction	compromised

The period in which Americans rebuilt the South after the Civil War was called

_____. The _____ of all slaves gave them their
5   **6**

freedom. Most people who served the Confederacy were forgiven by the United States

government and given _____. Reconstruction ended in 1877 when the
7

North and South _____ and agreed to let the South rejoin the United
8

States if African Americans were allowed to vote.

Word Challenge: Think About It

With a partner, take turns reading the sentences below out loud. Write a sentence to answer each question. The first one has been done for you.

1 Many people in the North worked for the **abolition** of slavery. How do you think they felt about slavery? _They wanted slavery to end._

2 The South **seceded** from the United States in 1861. How do you think the South felt about the United States? _____

_____

3 The **emancipation** of slaves took place after the Civil War. How do you think slaves felt about emancipation? _____

_____

4 Sumita **summarizes** textbook chapters after reading them. How do you think summarizing helps Sumita? _____

_____

Word Challenge: What's Your Answer?

Take turns with a partner reading each question out loud and writing an answer on the line. Answer the questions in complete sentences. The first one has been done for you.

1 Why would you and your friend agree to a **compromise**? _We would_ _agree to a compromise to end an argument._

2 What would you have done during **Reconstruction**? _____

_____

3 Why would you oppose **slavery**? _____

_____

4 What kind of words do you **abbreviate**? _____

_____

Synonyms or Antonyms

Look at each group of words below. Circle two words in each group that are synonyms or the two words that are antonyms. Then write *synonyms* or *antonyms* on the line.

1 emancipation   freedom

     abbreviate   reconstruction

_____

3 compromise   empire

     slavery   agreement

_____

2 summarize   constitution

     lengthen   judge

_____

4 reconstruction   export

     agriculture   rebuild

_____

Word Study: The Prefix *re-*

The prefix *re-* means *again* or *repeat*. It is often used with verbs, such as write. In some cases the new word can be both a noun and a verb.

rewrite (v.) to write something again
rewrite (n.) something that has been written again

A. Decide whether the word is a noun, a verb, or if it can be both. Write a definition for each.

	Noun, Verb, or Both?	Definition
1 reorganize		
2 reorder		
3 reconstruct		

B. Write a word from the chart that describes what is happening in the sentence.

1 _____ We need to order more pizzas for the party.

2 _____ The class organized its class library again.

54

The Language of Testing

How do you answer a question like this on a test?

Which of the following is correct?

    A. Americans own slaves today.
    B. People were elected to be slaves.
    C. Slaves did not have freedom.
    D. Most slaves lived in the North.

💡 **Tip**

The phrase *which of the following* means that you need to choose one of the answers (A, B, C, or D) to answer the question.

Test Strategy: Always read the whole question and the answers first. If the question has the phrase *which of the following* in it, ask the question in a different way. Start your question with *what, who* or *where*.

1 How would you write the question above in a different way?

_____

_____

Try the strategy again by asking these questions in a different way.

2 Which of the following served as President during the Civil War?

    A. Herbert Hoover
    B. Abraham Lincoln
    C. George Washington
    D. George Bush

3 Which of the following fought against the United States during the Civil War?

    A. China
    B. Confederacy
    C. Spain
    D. Britain

_____   _____

_____   _____

_____   _____

In Your Vocabulary Journal

Find each of these words in your American History Vocabulary Journal. Working by yourself or with a partner, use the definitions from pages 50 and 51 of your Work Text to complete the rest of the entry for each word.

abbreviation	**abolition**	**amnesty**	**compromise**	**confederacy**
emancipation	**reconstruction**	**secede**	**slavery**	**summarize**

Growth of American Industries

Read the passage below. Decide if each new word printed in **bold** is a noun or a verb. Write *noun* or *verb* near each word. Then use that information with other clues in the text to figure out what the new word means. The first one has been done for you.

The First Industrial Revolution

Vocabulary Strategy

Identify if a new word is used as a noun or a verb. Then use that information with other clues in the text to figure out what the new word means.

The Industrial Revolution began in America in 1790. It was a peaceful change from making goods by hand to **manufacturing**, or making goods by machines.

In 1790, machines that made **textiles**, or cloth, were built in America. The new machines were too large to be used at home, so **entrepreneurs** built factories. The location of rivers was one **factor** that helped entrepreneurs decide where to build factories. Factory owners used rivers to power the machines. They also used rivers to ship textiles to other places.

Factory owners wanted to produce large amounts of goods quickly. Producing large amounts

of a product at a time is known as mass production. An important step in mass production was to develop parts that could work in many products. These parts were called **interchangeable** parts.

After Americans learned to make interchangeable parts, they could make factory goods more quickly.

Interchangeable parts were first used to make guns for the army. Each gun was the same, so parts from one gun could be used to repair another. During the 1800s, America became a leader in manufacturing. This was largely the result of mass production and interchangeable parts.

✔ New American History Words

entrepreneur

   noun   a person who starts and runs a business

interchangeable

   adjective   something that can be used in place of something else

manufacturing

   noun   the process of making goods in a factory

   verb   making goods in a factory

textiles

   noun   cloth

Now read the passage below and practice the vocabulary strategy again. Write *noun* or *verb* above each new word printed in **bold**.

The Growth of Big Business

During the late 1800s, John D. Rockefeller became very rich by controlling America's oil business. At first Rockefeller owned just one oil company. He used his **capital**, or money he had earned from that business, to buy most of the nation's oil companies.

Rockefeller believed in a system called **capitalism**. This means the government allows people to own and control businesses.

In the late 1800s, most large businesses were organized as **corporations**. A corporation is a company that is often controlled by a group of people called a board of directors.

After Rockefeller gained control of many oil corporations, he formed a **trust**. A trust is a group of corporations that are controlled by one board of directors. Rockefeller could control the price of America's oil because he controlled the oil trust.

Many Americans said Rockefeller had too much control of the oil industry. They **concluded**, or decided, that laws were needed to control trusts and businesses. Congress passed new laws to control trusts.

More New American History Words

capital

noun   money or property used to start and run a business

capitalism

noun   a system in which the people of a country own businesses and earn profits

corporation

noun   a business or company

trust

noun   a group of corporations controlled by one organization

verb   to believe to be honest or dependable

Other Useful Words

conclude

verb   to make a decision based on known facts

factor

noun   something that affects a decision, an event, or what a person does

"Why do people think I'm rich? I own only one **trust**."

Apply the Strategy

Look at a chapter in your textbook that your teacher identifies. Identify the parts of speech of new words to help you figure out their meanings.

Matching

Finish the sentences in Group A with words from Group B. Write the letter of the word on the line. Discuss your choices with a partner.

Group A

1. We counted all our money and we _____ that we had enough to host a party.

2. Americans can own businesses because our country supports _____.

3. Our telephones were made with _____ parts.

4. I was known as an _____ when I started a successful business.

5. Many corporations were controlled by one _____.

Group B

A. capitalism

B. interchangeable

C. concluded

D. trust

E. entrepreneur

Group A

6. We need money or _____ to start a business.

7. Japanese companies are _____ fine cars.

8. Most clothing is made from _____.

9. Most department stores are run as _____.

10. The location of rivers was a _____ when deciding where to build factories.

Group B

F. corporations

G. manufacturing

H. factor

I. capital

J. textiles

Word Challenge: Would You Rather . . .

Take turns with a partner reading the statements below out loud. Think of a response and write it on the line. Explain your answers. The first one has been done for you.

1 Would you rather be an **entrepreneur** or work for a **corporation**? _I would rather_ _be an entrepreneur because I want to be my own boss._

2 Would you rather own a lot of **capital** or own a **trust**? _____

_____

3 Would you rather live under **capitalism** or another system? _____

_____

4 Would you rather **conclude** something based on facts or **factors**? _____

_____

Word Challenge: Finish the Idea

With a partner, take turns reading the incomplete sentences below. Write an ending for each. The first one has been done for you.

1 People might want to live in a country that allows **capitalism** because _____

Capitalism allows people to own their own businesses.

2 One **factor** for a good party is _____

_____

3 I want my business to be a **corporation** because _____

_____

4 I **concluded** that we had a good time on vacation because _____

_____

Extend the Meaning

Write the letter of the word or phrase that best completes each sentence. Discuss your choices with a partner.

1 You would use **textiles** to _____.
   a. bake a cake
   b. make a coat
   c. write a letter

2 **Manufacturing** could create _____.
   a. oranges
   b. computers
   c. flowers

3 You would probably find **interchangeable** parts on a _____.
   a. car
   b. apple
   c. banana

4 An **entrepreneur** might _____.
   a. shop in a department store
   b. study in college
   c. start a new supermarket

Word Study: The Suffix -able

When you add the suffix -able to a verb like *debate*, two things happen:
- The word becomes an adjective: *debatable*.
- The word now means "able to be debated."

Sometimes when a word ends with an *e*, you must drop the *e* before adding -able.

changeable (adj.) can be changed
washable (adj.) can be washed

A. Add the suffix -able to the words below and write a definition for each new word. Use a dictionary to check your spelling and definitions.

	+ -able	Definition
1 predict		
2 describe		
3 expand		
4 confirm		

B. Write sentences for two of the -able words from the chart.

1 _____

2 _____

The Language of Testing

How would you answer a question like this on a test?

What conclusion can be drawn about manufacturing textiles?

    A. The work should be done by hand.
    B. It is faster to make textiles by machine.
    C. People do not need textiles.
    D. All textiles are ugly.

Tip

When *what conclusion can be drawn* is used in a question, it means "what happened?" or "why did this happen?" You must choose the best possible reason from the choices.

Test Strategy: If the question has the phrase *what conclusion can be drawn* in it, rewrite it to ask *what happened*, or *why did this happen?*

1 How could you say the question above in a different way?

_____

_____

Try the strategy again by asking these questions in a different way.

2 John D. Rockefeller became rich from his oil business. What conclusion can be drawn about Rockefeller?

    A. Rockefeller had many friends.
    B. Rockefeller controlled most of America's oil.
    C. Rockefeller enjoyed traveling.
    D. Rockefeller's family was poor.

3 Factories were built near rivers. What conclusion can be made from this?

    A. Rivers were used to ship goods.
    B. Workers swam in the rivers.
    C. People fished in the rivers.
    D. River water was used to wash textiles.

_____   _____

_____   _____

_____   _____

In Your Vocabulary Journal

Find each of these words in your American History Vocabulary Journal. Working by yourself or with a partner, use the definitions from pages 56 and 57 of your Work Text to complete the rest of the entry.

capital	**capitalism**	**conclude**	**corporation**	**entrepreneur**
factor	**interchangeable**	**manufacturing**	**textile**	**trust**

Read the passage below. Think about the meanings of the new words printed in **bold**. Underline any examples or descriptions you find that might help you figure out the meaning of new words. Draw an arrow from the examples and descriptions to the word each describes. The first one has been done for you.

A Changing Nation

Vocabulary Strategy

Use examples and descriptions in the text to help you figure out the meanings of new words. Look for clues like *for example*, *like*, or *such as*. Look for pictures that might show what a new word means, too.

At the end of the 1800s, a group of people called **progressives** <u>wanted to help the nation make progress and solve problems in</u> American life.

The United States was changing in the late 1800s because of **immigration**, or the movement of people from many other countries into the country. Millions of poor immigrants started new lives in the United States. Some people called **nativists** were against immigration into the United States. They succeeded in having Congress pass laws limiting immigration.

By the late 1800s, the nation had many factories. Men, women, and children worked hard as factory workers, but they earned very little money. A number of people **analyzed**, or studied, the problems of poor workers. Some people thought that **socialism** might solve their problems. Under socialism, the government owns and controls all businesses. Capitalism won out, however. Progressives turned to other ideas to solve America's problems.

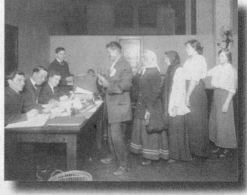

New American History Words

immigration

   noun   the act of moving into a new country

nativist

   noun   someone who is against people from other countries moving in

progressive

   noun   a person who wants to make society better

   adjective   having to do with improving things in a modern way

socialism

   noun   a system in which the government controls businesses and industries and all people are treated equally

Now read the passages below and practice the strategy again. Underline examples or descriptions in the passage. Draw arrows from the examples and descriptions to the new word each describes.

 ## Improving America

Another way the progressives tried to improve American life was through **conservation**, or protecting the land, air, and water. President Teddy Roosevelt was a Progressive. He worked with Congress to pass laws that created many national parks.

Teddy Roosevelt disliked trusts like the one that John D. Rockefeller controlled. Roosevelt believed they had too much control over American businesses. He acted on, or **responded** to, this problem by working with Congress. Laws were passed to break trusts up into smaller companies.

Segregation, the separation of people by race, was also a problem. In the South, African Americans had to use separate schools, parks, hospitals, and beaches. Some people began working for **integration**, allowing all races to use the same places.

Since the United States had first become a nation, women were not allowed to vote. But women across America worked hard to win **suffrage**, the right to vote. In 1920, the Nineteenth Amendment gave all women in the United States the right to vote.

 ### More New American History Words

conservation

noun saving and protecting the air, land, water, and resources

integration

noun to join together people of different races

segregation

noun the act of separating people by race

suffrage

noun the right to vote

 ### Other Useful Words

analyze

verb to study or think about something carefully in order to understand it

respond

verb to do or say something about what was done or said

Many people suffered for my **suffrage**. That's why I vote!

 ### Apply the Strategy

Look at a chapter in your textbook that your teacher identifies. Use examples, descriptions, and pictures in the text to help you figure out the meaning of any new words you find. You might also draw pictures to help you remember what new words mean.

Finish the Sentence

Use a word from the box to finish each sentence. Write the correct word on the line. Discuss your choices with a partner.

nativists	**analyzed**	**socialism**	**progressives**	**immigration**

1 During a period of _____ millions of people moved to America from Europe.

2 Americans called _____ did not want immigrants to come to America.

3 The economic system in which the government owns and controls industries and businesses is _____.

4 People who worked to improve society were _____.

5 In order to write a book report, I _____ the book carefully.

responded	**suffrage**	**conservation**	**integration**	**segregation**

6 Eric received a party invitation and _____ by saying he would be there.

7 People who protect the nation's air, land, and water care about _____.

8 Today, American men and women vote in elections because they all have _____.

9 At one time, African Americans had to use separate parks because of _____.

10 Students of all ethnicities now go to school together because of _____.

Word Challenge: What's Your Answer?

Take turns with a partner reading each question out loud and writing an answer on the line. Answer the questions in complete sentences. The first one has been done for you.

1 What kind of work would you do for **conservation**? _I would plant trees for_

conservation.

2 How would you **respond** if you won an award? _____

_____

3 What might you say to a **nativist**? _____

_____

4 What kind of problem would you need to **analyze**? _____

_____

Word Challenge: Word Associations

Take turns with a partner reading the group of words below. Write the word from the lesson that goes best with each group. The first one has been done for you.

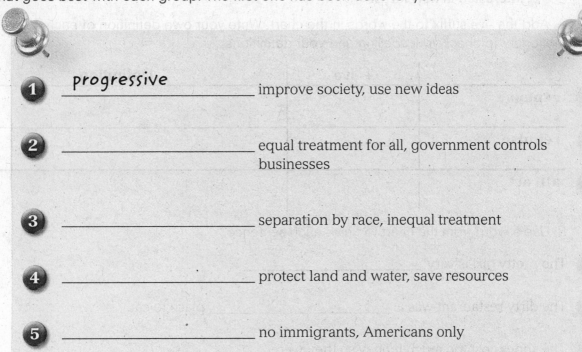

1 _progressive_ improve society, use new ideas

2 _____ equal treatment for all, government controls businesses

3 _____ separation by race, inequal treatment

4 _____ protect land and water, save resources

5 _____ no immigrants, Americans only

Finish the Idea

Finish each idea to make a complete sentence. Write your answer on the line. Discuss your answers with a partner.

1 I would be against **segregation** because _____

_____

2 American women wanted **suffrage** because _____

_____

3 I would have worked for **integration** in the United States because _____

_____

4 I would have helped the **progressives** because _____

_____

Word Study: The Suffix -ive

When you add the suffix *-ive* to a word like *progress,* two things happen:

- The suffix *-ive* turns the word into an adjective: *progressive.*
- The word now means "using or being interested in new ideas."

Some *-ive* words like *progressive* can also be nouns. A few other words like this are *representative, executive,* and *objective.*

A. Add the *-ive* suffix to the words in the chart. Write your own definition of each. Use a dictionary to check your spelling and your definitions.

	+ *-ive*	Definition
1 expense		
2 repulse		
3 attract		

B. Use a word from the chart to finish each sentence.

1 The pretty girl is very _____.

2 The dirty restaurant was a _____ place to eat.

3 The shoes cost too much money so they were _____.

The Language of Testing

What do you do when you read a question like this on a test?

Teddy Roosevelt was
most closely associated with

    A. conservation
    B. American Revolution
    C. Civil War
    D. Jamestown

💡 **Tip**

The phrase *most closely associated with* means you need to find the answer that has the closest connection to the person, event, or thing mentioned in the question.

> **Test Strategy:** If the question has the phrase *most closely associated with*, ask yourself which of the choices has the closest relationship to the question.

1 How could you say the question above in a different way?

_____

_____

Try the strategy again by asking these questions in a different way.

2 The period of immigration after 1870 was most closely associated with

    A. the building of new schools
    B. the end of slavery
    C. millions of people moving to America from Europe
    D. a boycott against Britain

3 The problem of segregation was most closely associated with

    A. building new roads
    B. the unfair treatment of African Americans
    C. women voting for president
    D. new factories in America

_____

_____

_____

_____

_____

_____

In Your Vocabulary Journal

Find each of these words in your American History Vocabulary Journal. Working by yourself or with a partner, use the definitions from pages 62 and 63 of your Work Text to complete the rest of the entry for each word.

analyze	**conservation**	**immigration**	**integration**	**nativist**
progressive	**respond**	**segregation**	**socialism**	**suffrage**

World War I

Read the passage below. Think about the meaning of the words printed in **bold**. Circle any words ending in *-ism*. Remember that *-ism* often refers to a belief or idea. Write near the circled words what you think they mean. The first one has been done for you.

Causes of World War I

Vocabulary Strategy

Use familiar prefixes and suffixes to help you understand the meaning of new words.

In 1914, most of Europe began fighting in a war that later came to be called World War I. During this war, Britain and France fought against Germany and Austria-Hungary. Other nations joined in as the war continued.

There were three major causes of the war. First, throughout Europe, there were strong feelings of

strong national feeling →

(nationalism.) Nationalism means people feel their country is the best. In Germany, nationalism made the government wish to control other nations.

A second cause of the war was **militarism**. Militarism means the building of strong armies. Militarism made countries believe that they could win control of others with their strong armies.

A third cause was **imperialism**. Imperialism means building an empire. Nations in Europe competed for colonies in Africa and Asia.

When World War I began, the United States believed in **isolationism**. The United States did not want to be part of the problems in Europe. However, newspapers **informed** Americans about the events of the war. This changed the public's feelings about the war. In 1917, the United States entered World War I to fight alongside Britain and France.

New American History Words

imperialism

noun   a belief that a strong nation builds and controls colonies

isolationism

noun   a nation's decision to not get involved with other countries

militarism

noun   the building of a powerful military that can be used for war

nationalism

noun   strong love for one's country and feeling that it is better than others

Now read the passage below and practice the strategy again. Circle any new words that contain familiar prefixes or suffixes that can help you figure out the meaning of new words.

The United States in World War I

In 1917, the United States began fighting against Germany and Austria-Hungary in World War I. The United States needed a large number of soldiers. The nation **mobilized**, or put together, its army. These soldiers went to Europe to fight in support of Britain and France. Some nations in Europe, such as Spain and Switzerland, were **neutral**, and did not fight during the war.

The United States helped Britain and France defeat Germany. On November 11, 1918, an **armistice** ended World War I.

The world had peace. The President of the United States, Woodrow Wilson, made a peace plan called the Fourteen Points. One of his points was that people should have **self-determination**, or control over their nation. Wilson **assumed**, or believed, that his peace plan would bring real peace to the world. By 1939, however, the world would be fighting in another terrible world war.

More New American History Words

armistice

noun   an agreement by enemy nations to stop fighting during a war

mobilize

verb   to prepare an army for war, or to organize support for a cause

neutral

adjective   a nation that does not help or support any nation fighting in a war

self-determination

noun   having free choice over one's state without outside control

Other Useful Words

assume

verb   to guess that something is true

inform

verb   to tell someone facts or to share information

What happened to **isolationism**?

It ended. We're **mobilized** to fight for Britain and France.

Apply the Strategy

Look at a chapter in your textbook that your teacher identifies. Use familiar prefixes and suffixes to help you figure out the meaning of any new words you find.

69

Finish the Sentence

Choose a word to finish each sentence. Write the correct word on the line. Discuss your choices with a partner.

1 Britain had many colonies because the nation believed in _____.

isolationism   **immigration**   **imperialism**

2 The United States did not want to fight in World War I because it believed in

_____.

isolationism   **immigration**   **imperialism**

3 Germany built a huge army because of _____.

isolationism   **militarism**   **reconstruction**

4 The Germans had strong feelings of _____ and believed their country

was the best.

militarism   **isolationism**   **nationalism**

5 Spain did not fight in World War I because it was a _____ nation.

neutral   **frontier**   **armistice**

6 The United States _____ the army to send soldiers to Europe.

mobilized   **informed**   **imported**

7 The newspapers _____ readers that the war had ended.

informed   **assumed**   **converted**

8 Mom always cooked meatballs on special days because she _____ it

was my favorite food.

informed   **assumed**   **converted**

Word Challenge: True or False

Take turns with a partner reading the sentences below out loud. Write **T** next to each sentence that is true. Write **F** next to each sentence that is false. Rewrite the false sentences. The first one has been done for you.

1. __F__ **Militarism** means an agreement to stop fighting.

   Militarism means to build an army.

2. _____ If a nation is **neutral**, it will fight in a war.

   _____

3. _____ **Imperialism** means building colonies and an empire.

   _____

4. _____ **Self-determination** means to organize soldiers for war.

   _____

Word Challenge: Which Word?

With a partner, take turns saying the words listed below. Together, think of a statement for each one that gives a clue about its meaning. Write your statement next to the word. The first one has been done for you.

1. **inform** _"I share information."_____

2. **isolationism** _____

3. **armistice** _____

4. **assume** _____

5. **mobilize** _____

Finish the Idea

Finish each idea to make a complete sentence. Write your answer on the line. Discuss your answers with a partner.

1 If you lived in a **neutral** nation, you might _____

_____

2 A nation would sign an **armistice** if _____

_____

3 I would **assume** you are happy if _____

_____

4 You would show feelings of **nationalism** if _____

_____

Word Study: The Suffix -ize

When you add -ize to an adjective such as custom, two things happen:

- The word becomes a verb: customize.
- The word now means to make something for one's own special taste.

custom (adj.) something made to personal order
customize (v.) to make something for one's own special taste

Add the suffix -ize to the words below. Write your own definition for each word. Use a dictionary to check your spelling and your definitions.

	+ -ize	Definition
1 mobile		
2 military		
3 neutral		
4 civil		
5 revolution		

The Language of Testing

How would you answer a question like this on a test?

What was one **major cause** of World War I?

    A. imperialism
    B. slavery
    C. the search for gold
    D. emancipation

 Tip

The word *cause* means the reason why something happened. The *major cause* is the most important reason why something happened.

Test Strategy: If a question asks for the major cause of something, restate the question using the *phrase most important reason for*. You can also add the phrase *is a major cause of* to each answer choice to test if it is right or wrong. For example, *imperialism* was a major cause of World War I.

1 How could you say the question above in a different way?

_____

_____

Try the strategy again by asking these questions in a different way. Also write what phrase you would use to test the answer choices.

2 Ana was an excellent student. What was the major cause for her success in school?

    A. She wore nice clothes.
    B. She had a cell phone.
    C. She studied for every test.
    D. She liked to sing.

3 Bob's new shoe store went out of business. What was the major cause of Bob's store closing?

    A. Bob was very friendly.
    B. The shoes cost too much money.
    C. The shoes were beautiful.
    D. The store had shoes and sneakers.

_____   _____

_____   _____

_____   _____

In Your Vocabulary Journal

Find each of these words in your American History Vocabulary Journal. Working by yourself or with a partner, use the definition from pages 68 and 69 of your Work Text to complete the rest of the entry for each word.

armistice	**assume**	**imperialism**	**inform**	**isolationism**
militarism	**mobilize**	**nationalism**	**neutral**	**self-determination**

Read the first passage below. Underline any examples or descriptions you find that might help you figure out the meaning of new words. Draw an arrow from the examples and descriptions to the word each describes. The first one has been done for you.

After World War I

After World War I, all the fighting nations signed a peace treaty. That treaty **specified**, or named, Germany as the nation that started the war. It also punished Germany for starting the war. Germany was forced to pay **reparations** of billions of dollars to Britain and France.

Many of the nations who fought wanted to prevent future wars. To do so, they followed a policy of **disarmament**. While the United States began making and owning fewer weapons, however, other countries like Germany began rebuilding their armies.

To many Americans, the 1920s were good years. Many people had more money and more time away from work. But some Americans were unhappy and left the United States. They settled in Europe and were called **expatriates**.

In 1919, the **Prohibition** Amendment was added to the Constitution. It said it was against the law to make or drink alcoholic beverages. It was impossible to carry out this law, however. In 1933, another amendment ended Prohibition forever.

Vocabulary Strategy

Use examples and descriptions to help you figure out the meaning of new words. Look for clues such as *like*, *for example*, and *such as*. Look for pictures that might show you what a word means, too.

New American History Words

disarmament

noun   when a nation makes and owns fewer weapons

expatriate

noun   someone who has left his or her own country to live and work in another country

prohibition

noun   the time during which something popular is made illegal, or the period in the United States when alcoholic beverages were illegal

reparation

noun   money that a nation that has lost a war must pay the winning countries

Now read the passage below and practice the strategy again. Underline the examples and descriptions in the passage. Draw an arrow from each to the word it describes.

Difficult Times in America

During the 1920s, many Americans wanted to stop immigration. Congress passed a law creating **quotas**. The quotas said how many people could come to America from different countries each year. The quotas allowed fewer immigrants from eastern and southern Europe.

In 1929, the Great **Depression** began. The main events of the Great Depression can be **sequenced** in the order that they happened. First, the stock market crashed and millions of people became poor. Second, more and more people continued to lose their jobs. Third, Franklin D. Roosevelt was elected President. Fourth, the President started new programs to end the Depression.

President Roosevelt started **relief**, or help, programs for people who did not have jobs. His programs gave jobs to millions of people. The new programs made the United States a **welfare** state. A welfare state provides certain things to people when they cannot find jobs.

More New American History Words

depression

noun   a time when spending is low and many people do not have jobs

quota

noun   the number that is a goal, like a limit on the number of immigrants or how many items should be made or sold

relief

noun   help for serious problems

welfare

noun   being happy, healthy, and comfortable, or money the government gives people to help them survive

Other Useful Words

sequence

noun   the order in which things should be

verb   to put things in order so that one thing comes after another

specify

verb   to name something

Apply the Strategy

Look at a chapter in your textbook that your teacher identifies. Use examples, descriptions, and pictures to help you figure out the meaning of any new words you find.

Find the Word

Write a word from the box next to each clue. Then write the word made by the boxed letters to answer the question below.

expatriates	welfare	depression	prohibition	quota
sequence	relief	disarmament	specify	reparations

1. when people do not have jobs __ __ __ ☐ __ __ __ __

2. help for a serious problem __ __ ☐ __ __ __

3. money paid by a country __ __ __ ☐ __ __ __ __ __ __ __

4. to make fewer weapons __ __ __ __ __ ☐ __ __ __ __ __

5. people who live and work in another country __ __ __ __ ☐ __ __ __ __ __ __

6. government money that helps people __ __ __ __ __ __ ☐ __ __

7. when something is illegal __ __ __ __ __ __ ☐ __ __ __ __

8. to name something __ __ __ __ ☐ __ __

9. an amount that is a goal __ __ __ __ ☐ __

10. an order of events __ __ __ __ ☐ __ __ __ __

What did Germany have to pay after World War I?

It paid __ __ __ __ __ __ __ __ __ __ __ __ S .

Word Challenge: Word Association

Take turns with a partner reading the groups of words below. Write the word from the lesson that goes best with each group. The first one has been done for you.

1 ___prohibition___ not allowed, illegal, stop

2 _____ amount, limit, goal

3 _____ help, support, assistance

4 _____ place in order, set of events

5 _____ government money, help, well-being

Word Challenge: What's Your Reason?

Take turns with a partner reading the statements below out loud. Think of a reason for each statement and write it on the line. Write your reasons in complete sentences. The first one has been done for you.

1 It would have been hard to live during the Great **Depression**. _It was hard_ _because no one had any money to buy food._

2 I would **specify** my favorite foods when visiting a friend for dinner. _____

_____

3 I would **sequence** the party pictures in the order that they were taken. _____

_____

4 I feel **relief** at the end of the school year. _____

_____

Extend the Meaning

Write the letter of the word or phrase that best completes each sentence. Discuss your choices with a partner.

1 A country that wants **disarmament** would _____.
  a. build more weapons
  b build fewer weapons
  c. want a huge army

2 It is not possible to **sequence** _____.
  a. numbers
  b. dates
  c. pencils

3 During a **depression**, most people become _____.
  a. richer
  b. smarter
  c. poorer

4 An American **expatriate** might live in _____.
  a. New York
  b. California
  c. France

Word Study: The Suffix -ment

When the suffix -ment is added to a word like settle, two things happen:
  • The suffix -ment changes a verb into a noun: settlement.
  • The word now names the result or process of settling.

settle (v.) to set up a home somewhere
settlement (n.) a community built by people just moving into the area, or the process of moving into an area.

A. Add the suffix -ment to the words below. Write your own definition for each word. Use a dictionary to check your spelling and definitions.

	+ -ment	Definition
1 achieve		
2 move		
3 ship		
4 develop		

B. Complete each sentence with a word from the chart.

1 Roberto's excellent grades were an _____.

2 We could feel the _____ of the ship as we sailed.

78

The Language of Testing

How would you answer a question like this on a test?

The difficult times of the Great Depression (led to)

    A. the beginning of World War I.
    B. too many people out of work.
    C. new libraries being built.
    D. Americans moving to China.

> 💡 **Tip**
>
> The phrase *led to* tells you that you need to find a result of the event in the question.

Test Strategy: Always read the whole question and all the answers first. Then if the question has the phrase *led to*, reword the question to ask for a result of the event in the question.

1 How could you say the question above in a different way?

_____

_____

Try the strategy again by asking these questions in a different way.

2 Paul's job in a summer camp led to

    A. an interest in becoming a teacher.
    B. a dislike for horses.
    C. being afraid of dogs.
    D. learning to cook.

_____

_____

_____

3 Germany's defeat in World War I led to

    A. fifty years of peace.
    B. more trips to Germany.
    C. Germany paying reparations.
    D. the building of new museums.

_____

_____

_____

In Your Vocabulary Journal

Find each of these words in your American History Vocabulary Journal. Working by yourself or with a partner, use the definitions from pages 74 and 75 of your Work Text to complete the rest of the entry for each word.

depression	**disarmament**	**expatriate**	**prohibition**	**quota**
relief	**reparation**	**sequence**	**specify**	**welfare**

World War II

Read the passage below. Think about the meanings of the new words printed in **bold**. Circle any familiar root words inside the new words that might help you figure out what these words mean. The first one has been done for you.

World War II Begins

Vocabulary Strategy

Use words you know to help unlock unfamiliar words in the same family. For example, *total* can help you unlock the meaning of *totalitarianism*.

A **survey** of the 1930s and 1940s tells us that these were difficult years in Europe. Italy and Germany had governments that were based on ideas of **Fascism**. Under Fascism, powerful leaders had strong armies and full control of the government.

The governments of Italy, Germany, the Soviet Union and Japan were also based on the ideas of **totalitarianism**. These governments had total control over the lives of every person. People who spoke out against the government were killed.

Adolf Hitler became the fascist leader of Germany. In 1936, he began taking control of different countries in Europe. At first, Britain and France followed a policy of **appeasement**, or giving in, to Hitler. World War II began in 1939 when Hitler's army attacked Poland. Britain and France fought against Hitler as Poland's **allies**, or friends. However, Hitler quickly won control of Poland.

There was a quick increase, or **escalation**, in fighting. Hitler won control of many other countries, including France.

Adolf Hitler

New American History Words

ally

noun   a person or country that agrees to support another

appeasement

noun   the act of giving in to a person or country to have peace

escalation

noun   a sudden and large increase

facism

noun   a government that controls the lives of people, targets certain groups, and builds a large army

totalitarianism

noun   a form of government, such as fascism, that has total control over the lives of people

Now read the passage below and practice the vocabulary strategy again. Circle familiar root words that are found in larger, unfamiliar words.

Winning World War II

On December 7, 1941, Japan bombed American ships at Pearl Harbor in Hawaii and killed more than 2,000 Americans. After that, the United States went to war against Japan, Germany, and Italy. In 1942, all Japanese Americans on the West Coast were ordered to move to **internment** camps. These camps were heavily guarded.

The United States and its allies defeated Germany, Italy, and Japan in 1945. The world soon learned about the **Holocaust**, or the organized killing of six million Jews in Europe. As Hitler captured different countries, Jews and other people were sent to death camps. Hitler carefully planned this **genocide** against the Jews.

At the end of World War II, American soldiers started the **liberation** of the camps. However, it was too late to save the millions who had already been killed.

More New American History Words

genocide

noun   the killing of an entire race or group

Holocaust

noun   the murder of six million Jews by Hitler during World War II

noun   total or near total destruction of life

internment

noun   the act of forcing people to stay in one place, such as a prison or a guarded space

liberation

noun   the act of freeing people

Other Useful Words

highlight

verb   to show that something is important

noun   an important time during an event

survey

noun   the information that is gathered about a topic

verb   to collect information about a topic

Apply the Strategy

Look at a chapter in your textbook that your teacher identifies. Use familiar root words to help you figure out the meaning of any new words you find.

Finish the Sentence

Use a word from the box to finish each sentence. Write the correct word on the line. Discuss your choices with a partner.

survey	genocide	appeasement	escalation	fascism

1. The form of government in which a leader uses the army to control the country is _____.

2. A _____ was made before the election to find out how people planned to vote.

3. More and more soldiers died because of the _____ in fighting.

4. Tommy's mother let him eat too many cookies because she hoped _____ would stop him from fighting with his brother.

5. Hitler committed _____ against many groups, including the Jews.

Holocaust	Totalitarianism	liberated	internment	highlight

6. Jenna uses a yellow marker to _____ important ideas as she reads.

7. Japanese Americans were forced into _____ camps during World War II.

8. The killing of six million Jews during World War II was the _____.

9. _____ means a government that has total control over the lives of people.

10. The death camps were _____ at the end of the war.

82

Word Challenge: What's Your Answer?

Take turns with a partner reading each question out loud and writing an answer on the line. Answer questions in complete sentences. The first one has been done for you.

1 Why would you not want to live under **fascism**? _I would not like to live_ _under fascism because I like having freedom._

2 What would you **highlight** in your history book? _____

_____

3 What could you learn if you took a **survey** in your school? _____

_____

4 Why is **genocide** very wrong? _____

_____

Word Challenge: True or False

Take turns with a partner reading the sentences below out loud. Write **T** next to each sentence that is true. Write **F** next to each sentence that is false. Rewrite the false sentences. The first one has been done for you.

1 __F__ **Holocaust** is the name of a fascist leader.

The Holocaust was the murder of six million Jews during WW II.

2 _____ Under **totalitarianism**, a government has total control over people's lives.

_____

3 _____ **Liberation** means that people must stay in prison.

_____

4 _____ **Escalation** means there would be less fighting during a war.

_____

Synonyms and Antonyms

Look at each group of words. Circle two words in each group that are synonyms or two words in each group that are antonyms. Then write whether the circled words are synonyms or antonyms on the line below each group.

1
| liberation | suffrage |
| neutral | freedom |

_____

3
| survey | region |
| study | duties |

_____

2
| escalation | lowering |
| compromise | slavery |

_____

4
| highlight | canal |
| charter | emphasize |

_____

Word Study: Compound Words

A compound word is a word that is made when two words are joined together. The new word often has a completely new meaning from the words it contains.

birth + place = birthplace
fire + works = fireworks

A. Complete the chart.

	Compound Word	Definition
1 high + light		
2 sky + scraper		
3 home + land		

B. Complete each sentence with a compound word from the chart.

1 Alexandra's _____ is in Mexico and she has always lived there.

2 The tall _____ had more than 100 floors.

84

The Language of Testing

How would you answer a question like this on a test?

What would be the best title for a newspaper story about the internment of Japanese Americans during World War II?

- A. Japanese Americans Live in California
- B. Japanese Americans are Unfairly Sent to Internment Camps
- C. Japanese Americans Shop for Food
- D. Japanese Americans Move to China

Tip

The phrase *what would be the best title* means you must think of the most important idea about the topic.

Test Strategy: If the question asks *what would be the best title*, ask yourself which of the four choices shows the most important idea about the topic. That will be the correct answer for the question.

Try the strategy again with these questions. Circle the best answer and write a sentence to explain your choice.

1 What would be the best title for an article about the celebration of Thanksgiving?

- A. Too Many Fish
- B. Too Far to Drive
- C. A Holiday for All Americans
- D. No School on Thursday

2 What would be the best title for an article about U.S. entry into World War II?

- A. The United States Enters the War After Pearl Harbor
- B. Hitler Speaks to Germany
- C. Fascism in Italy
- D. Not Enough Food

_____   _____

_____   _____

_____   _____

In Your Vocabulary Journal

Find each of these words in your American History Vocabulary Journal. Working by yourself or with a partner, use the definitions from pages 80 and 81 of your Work Text to complete the rest of the entry for each word.

ally   appeasement   escalation   fascism   genocide   highlight

Holocaust   internment   liberation   survey   totalitarianism

Lesson 15
The Cold War to the Present

Read the passage below. Think about the meanings of the words printed in **bold**. Underline any definitions that might help you figure out what these words mean. The first one has been done for you.

The Cold War Years

Vocabulary Strategy

Look for definitions to help you understand the meanings of new words.

The Cold War began in 1945. It was a struggle between the United States and the Soviet Union.

The Soviet Union had a totalitarian government that followed the ideas of **communism**. Under communism, the government owns all land and businesses. The Soviet Union wanted to spread communism to other countries. The United States responded with a policy of **containment**. This policy means working to stop the spread of communism.

Today, when people **review**, or study, the Cold War years, they learn that Americans worried about the spread of communism. They also worried that the Soviet Union would attack America with **nuclear** weapons. Both nations had nuclear weapons, however, and they agreed to not use them.

During the 1950s, African Americans worked to end **discrimination**, unfair treatment because of race. Through many protests and battles, African Americans slowly won equal rights.

New American History Words

communism

noun   a system of government in which the government controls all businesses, or an economy in which there is no government and the people share the wealth

containment

noun   the policy of working to stop the spread of something

discrimination

noun   the unfair treatment of people because of their race, age, religion, or other factors

nuclear

adjective   powered by the energy that is given off by splitting atoms

Now read this passage and practice the vocabulary strategy again. Underline any definitions in the passage that help you figure out what the new words in **bold** mean.

Some Problems in Today's World

The United States has had a huge **deficit**. A deficit means the government spends more money than it takes in.

The United States has fought two wars against the Middle East country of Iraq. During the 1990s, American leaders believed Iraq was building very dangerous weapons. **Sanctions** were placed against Iraq. This means nations could not trade with Iraq. In 2003, the United States and Great Britain went to war against Iraq. Iraq's leader, Saddam Hussein, was removed from power. The sanctions were lifted.

Iraq could trade with other nations again. But problems in Iraq still continue.

Terrorism is a world problem. The worst act of terrorism in the United States happened on September 11, 2001. Terrorists attacked the World Trade Center in New York City and the Pentagon building in Washington, D.C. More than 3,000 people were killed. People everywhere **related** to the pain felt by the victims and their families. President George W. Bush promised there would be **retaliation**, or fighting back.

More New American History Words

deficit

   noun   the government's spending of more money than it takes in

retaliation

   noun   the act of taking action against a person or country that has hurt you

sanctions

   noun   a decision to stop trade with a nation that has caused problems

terrorism

   noun   unpredictable acts of violence against innocent people to make a statement

Other Useful Words

relate

   verb   to feel connected to or to respond to something

review

   verb   to study or examine something

   noun   the act of studying or analyzing something

Of course there's a **deficit**. You're spending more that you make.

Apply the Strategy

Look at a chapter in your textbook that your teacher identifies. Use definitions in the text to help you figure out the meaning of any new words you find.

Finish the Sentence

Choose a word to finish each sentence. Write the correct word on the line. Discuss your choices with a partner.

1 The _____ weapons are very, very dangerous.

    survey   **nuclear**   **review**

2 People who live under _____ are not allowed to have their own businesses.

    republic   **communism**   **mercantilism**

3 A good student always _____ before a test.

    reviews   **expands**   **sequences**

4 If you spend more money than you earn, you will have a _____.

    sanction   **review**   **deficit**

5 Dan did not do well in sports so he could _____ to other people who were also not good athletes.

    review   **relate**   **retaliate**

6 The United States had a policy of _____ against communism.

    containment   **quota**   **terrorism**

7 The attacks on the World Trade Center and the Pentagon on September 11, 2001, were an example of _____.

    deficit   **terrorism**   **communism**

8 African Americans faced _____ when they were not allowed to buy houses in white neighborhoods.

    liberation   **discrimination**   **depression**

9 Many nations did not trade with Iraq because of _____ against that country.

    surveys   **reviews**   **sanctions**

10 The United States attacked terrorist bases in _____ for the World Trade Center attacks.

    retaliation   **liberation**   **escalation**

World Challenge: Which Word?

With a partner, take turns saying the words listed below. Together, think of a statement for each one that gives a clue about its meaning. Write your statement next to the word. The first one has been done for you.

1 deficit _"I am a problem with money."_

2 communism _____

3 discrimination _____

4 retaliation _____

Word Challenge: Think About It

With a partner, take turns reading the sentences below out loud. Write a sentence to answer each question. The first one has been done for you.

1 African Americans faced **discrimination** when they applied for jobs. Do you think they were treated fairly? _No. Everyone should have the same chances to get a job._

2 Sam did not **review** for his test. How do you think Sam did on the test?

_____

_____

3 The U.S. government has **sanctions** against a certain country. How do you think the U.S. government feels about that country? _____

_____

4 Meena **relates** to Sung because he hates big parties. Do you think Meena would rather go to a large party or a small one? _____

_____

Finish the Idea

Finish each idea to make a complete sentence. Write your answers on the line. Discuss your answers with a partner.

1 I would work to end **discrimination** because _____

_____

2 **Communism** is different from capitalism because _____

_____

3 A **deficit** can be a problem because _____

_____

4 **Nuclear** weapons are dangerous because _____

_____

Word Study: The Suffix -ed

The suffix -ed changes a verb to the past tense.
- Present tense: Peter *reviews* the lesson.
- Past tense: Martha *reviewed* the lesson.

The suffix -ed is added only to verbs.
When -ed is added to a verb that ends in y, change the y to i and then add -ed.
inform = informed
specify = specified

A. Complete the chart.

	Present Tense	+ -ed	Definition
1	review		
2	contain		
3	discriminate		
4	specify		

B. Use a past tense word from the chart to finish each sentence.

1 When I ordered the sandwich, I _____ that I wanted whole wheat bread.

2 The small box _____ a beautiful watch.

The Language of Testing

How would you answer a question like this on a test?

Which point of view did the U.S. government have about communism during the Cold War?

A. Communism is good for poor people.
B. All people in Europe should follow communism.
C. We should contain communism.
D. Communism will soon end.

 Tip

The phrase *which point of view* means you must decide on the point of view of one person or group. Different people or groups will often have different points of view about the same event.

Test Strategy: Always begin by reading the full question and all of the possible answers. Then think of at least two different points of view for the same event. Decide on the one point of view from the answer group that is probably held by the person or group named in the question.

Try the strategy again with these questions. Circle the answer you think is correct. Write a sentence to explain why you chose your answer.

1 The school principal said students will fail if they miss more than ten days of school. The principal's point of view is that

A. students can learn well at home.
B. too many students are promoted.
C. school attendance is important.
D. students should ride bikes.

_____

_____

_____

2 What was President George W. Bush's point of view about the terrorist attacks on September 11, 2001?

A. We should forget about the attacks.
B. We should retaliate.
C. We cannot prevent terrorism.
D. The attacks were an accident.

_____

_____

_____

In Your Vocabulary Journal

Find each of these words in your American History Vocabulary Journal. Working by yourself or with a partner, use the definitions on pages 86 and 87 of your Work Text to complete the rest of the entry for each word.

communism	**containment**	**deficit**	**discrimination**	**nuclear**
relate	**retaliation**	**review**	**sanctions**	**terrorism**

Glossary

Aa

abbreviate (uh **bree** vee **ayt**)
noun   to shorten (*Ali had to* **abbreviate** *most of the words so they would fit on the paper.*)

abolition (**ab** uh **lish** uhn)
noun   the act of ending something, especially slavery (*Americans who hated slavery worked for its* **abolition.**)

agriculture (**ag** ri **kuhl** chuhr)
noun   farming and ranching (*Jim enjoyed doing farm chores and wanted to work in* **agriculture.**)

amendment (uh **mend** muhnt)
noun   a law that is added to the Constitution, or a change that is made to make a law or rule better (*An* **amendment** *was added to the school's rules so that trips can end after school hours.*)

ally (**al** eye)
noun   a person or country that agrees to support another (*The two nations became* **allies** *after signing the treaty.*)

amnesty (**am** nuhs tee)
noun   government forgiveness of crimes (*Most Southern soldiers received* **amnesty** *and were not punished for fighting the Civil War.*)

analyze (an **uh** lyz)
verb   to study or think about something carefully in order to understand it (*I* **analyzed** *the difficult math problem and then found a way to solve it.*)

appeasement (uh **peez** muhnt)
noun   the act of giving in to a person or country to have peace (*France thought that the* **appeasement** *of Hitler would keep peace in Europe but it brought war instead.*)

apprentice (uh **prehn** tis)
noun   a young person who works without pay to learn a job (*Ben Franklin learned to be a printer by working as an* **apprentice** *in a print shop.*)

armistice (**ahr** muh stis)
noun   an agreement by enemy nations to stop fighting during a war (*Americans were happy when an* **armistice** *ended the fighting of World War I.*)

artifacts (**ahrt** uh fakts)
noun   tools and objects made by people (**Artifacts** *like knives and spears tell us about the tools people made long ago.*)

assembly (uh **sehm** blee)
noun   a group of individuals who are chosen by the people to make laws (*The town formed an* **assembly** *to make laws.*)

assume (uh **soom**)
verb   to guess that something is true (*Chan* **assumed** *he would be elected president because of his popularity.*)

Bb

border (**bawr** duhr)
noun   an imaginary line that divides states or countries (*She lives near the* **border** *between Mexico and Texas.*)

boycott (**boy** kaht)
verb   to refuse to buy certain goods or services (*They decided to* **boycott** *the newspaper after the price went up.*)

noun   the act of refusing to buy certain goods or services (*There was a* **boycott** *on all fur coats by the animal activists.*)

Cc

canal (kuh **nal**)
noun   an artificial waterway (*The Erie* **Canal** *allowed ships to travel from Buffalo to New York City.*)

capital (**kap** uht uhl)
noun   money or property used to start and run a business (*Mike had saved money for a few years so he had enough* **capital** *to open a clothing store.*)

capitalism (**kap** uht uhl **iz** uhm)

noun   a system in which people of a country own businesses and earn profits (*Pam wanted her own business so she moved to a country that allowed* **capitalism***.*)

charter (**chahrt** uhr)

noun   a document that allows a business, settlement, or government to exist (*The settlers were thankful when they received the* **charter***.*)

civilization (**siv** uh luh **zay** shuhn)

noun   a group of people who share the same art, history and laws (*The Native American* **civilization** *in the Northwest included religious beliefs and special music.*)

colony (**kahl** uh nee)

noun   a settlement that belongs to another country (*The* **colony** *was within their boundary, but it was not theirs.*)

communism (**kahm** yoo **niz** uhm)

noun   a system of government in which the government controls all businesses, or an economy in which there is no government and the people share the wealth (***Communism** made it hard for most people in the Soviet Union to own a car.*)

compromise (**kahm** pruh myz)

verb   to give up something to end an argument (*Jenny* **compromised** *with her brother about the TV.*)

noun   an agreement reached when both sides give up something they want to solve an argument (*Michael agreed to a* **compromise** *with Jim.*)

conclude (kuhn **klood**)

verb   to make a decision based on known facts (*Liz* **concluded** *from the news that it was a bad time to go to Florida.*)

Confederacy (kuhn **fehd** uhr uh see)

noun   a group of states or people with the same goals, or the group of states that broke away from the United States in 1860-1861 (*Some Native American nations formed a* **confederacy** *to help each other.*)

confirm (kuhn **furm**)

verb   to prove or show that information is true (*Sofia was asked to* **confirm** *her place of birth.*)

congress (**kahng** gruhs)

noun   a large meeting held to make decisions about laws and government, or the lawmaking branch of the United States government (*American leaders met at their first* **Congress** *in Philadelphia.*)

conservation (**kahn** suhr **vay** shuhn)

noun   saving and protecting the air, land, water and resources (*President Teddy Roosevelt cared about* **conservation** *so he created national parks.*)

containment (kuhn **tayn** muhnt)

noun   the policy of working to stop the spread of something (*America had a* **containment** *policy towards Japan after WWII.*)

contrast (**kahn** trast)

noun   the differences between things (*There was a* **contrast** *in the behavior of the people before and after the Depression.*)

verb   to compare the differences between things (*We were asked to compare and* **contrast** *two different colonies.*)

convert (kuhn **vurt**)

verb   to change beliefs or to change form (*Ted* **converted** *to Judaism when he married his wife.*)

(kahn **vurt**)

noun   someone who has changed his or her beliefs (*The former Baptist is a* **convert** *to Catholicism.*)

corporation (**kawr** puh ray shuhn)

noun   a business or company (*Most large U.S. businesses are* **corporations***.*)

covenant (**kuhv** uh nuhnt)

noun   a promise or a written agreement (*After they signed the* **covenant***, the two countries became allies.*)

culture (**kuhl** chuhr)

noun   a body of shared traditions and beliefs (*Gabriel asked his father teach him about the Columbian* **culture***.*)

Dd

debate (dee **bayt**)

verb   to discuss a topic from different points of view (*Manuel wanted to* **debate** *politics with the unfair leader.*)

(di bayt)

noun   a discussion in which people argue different points of view (*During the* **debate**, *Alexi got so angry his face turned red.*)

deficit (dehf fuh sit)

noun   the government's spending of more money than it takes in (*The United Sates has a* **deficit** *because it spends more money than it takes in.*)

define (dee **fyn**)

verb   to explain what something means (*I use a dictionary to help me* **define** *the meaning of new words.*)

democracy (di **mahk** ruh see)

noun   a system of government in which people choose their leaders and laws (*Americans are grateful to live in a* **democracy**.)

Depression (dee **prehsh** uhn)

noun   a time when spending is low and many people do not have jobs (*Karen's parents lost their jobs during the* **Depression**.)

describe (di **skryb**)

verb   to tell what something is like (*Jessica* **described** *the color and shape of the pockets on her jeans.*)

disarmament (dis **ahr** muh muhnt)

noun   when a nation makes and owns fewer weapons (*The United States had agreed to* **disarmament** *so it made fewer weapons after World War I.*)

discrimination (di **skrim** ih **nay** shuhn)

noun   the unfair treatment of people because of their race, age, religion or other factors (**Discrimination** *against senior citizens made it hard for them to get jobs.*)

dissenter (di **sehnt** uhr)

noun   a person who disagrees (*With so many* **dissenters** *in the group, there was sure to be an argument.*)

doctrine (**dahk** trin)

noun   a statement of important beliefs (*The school's* **doctrine** *includes kindness to all people.*)

domesticate (doh **mehs** ti **kayt**)

verb   to tame animals and grow plants for human use (*Maria's mother made her* **domesticate** *the new dog before he was allowed to live indoors.*)

duties (**doot** ees)

noun   jobs and responsibilities, or taxes on goods brought into a country (*The teacher's* **duties** *included preparing tests, and teaching classes.*)

Ee

emancipation (ee **mahn** suh **pay** shun)

noun   freedom from something unpleasant, especially slavery (*The Thirteenth Amendment required the* **emancipation** *of all slaves.*)

emphasize (**ehm** fuh **syz**)

verb   to show that something is very important (*The teacher* **emphasized** *that all students must obey the rules.*)

empire (**ehm pyr**)

noun   a group of nations that are ruled by a more powerful country (*Peru, Ecuador, and Chile were in the same* **empire**.)

enterprise (**ehnt** uhr **pryz**)

noun   a business undertaking or new project (*Eman was certain that her* **enterprise** *would be a success.*)

entrepreneur (**ahn** truh pruh **nur**)

noun.   a person who starts and runs a business (*Julie was an* **entrepreneur** *who built the first jewelry store here.*)

environment (ehn **vy** ruhn muhnt)

noun   the land, plants, and animals in an area (*The cactus can live many years in a desert, or dry* **environment**.)

escalation (**ehs** kuh **lay** shuhn)

noun   a sudden and large increase (*The* **escalation** *of the fighting meant many more soldiers would be hurt.*)

exchange (ehks **chaynj**)

verb   to swap or to trade (*Fred* **exchanged** *blankets for some food.*)

noun   a swap or trade (*There was a friendly* **exchange** *of jewelry between the two merchants.*)

executive (eg **zehk** yoo tiv)

adjective having to do with putting laws into action (*The principal made an **executive** decision to ban gum chewing in school.*)

expand (ehk **spand**)

verb to make something larger (*The store owner **expanded** the size of the store.*)

expansion (ehk **span** shuhn)

noun the act of growing larger (*As the family grew larger, the house needed an **expansion**.*)

expatriate (ehks **pay** tree it)

noun someone who has left his or her own country to live and work in another country (*Some American **expatriates** lived in France.*)

expedition (ehks puh **dish** uhn)

noun a group that makes a trip for a specific reason, or a journey of exploration (*The Lewis and Clark **expedition** explored the land of the Louisiana Purchase.*)

export (ek **spawrt**)

verb to sell goods to another country (*The United States **exports** many cars to other nations.*)

noun an item sold to another country (*The United States sent a big shipment of **exports** overseas.*)

Ff

factor (**fak** tuhr)

noun something that affects a decision, an event, or what a person does (*The cold snowy winters were the **factor** that made Lori decide to buy warm boots.*)

Fascism (**fash iz** uhm)

noun a government that controls the lives of people, targets certain groups, and builds a large army (*Mussolini believed in **Fascism** and built a large army in Italy.*)

federalism (**fehd** uhr uhl **iz** uhm)

noun sharing of powers between the state government and the national government (***Federalism** allows the federal government to have an army and the state governments make school laws.*)

frontier (fruhn **tihr**)

noun the outer edge of settled land (*Americans moved west to start new homes on the **frontier**.*)

Gg

genocide (**jehn** uh **syd**)

noun the killing of an entire race or group (***Genocide** took place in Rwanda when one group tried to kill all the people in another group.*)

Hh

highlight (**hy lyt**)

verb to show that something is important (*My mother **highlights** the importance of drinking milk every day.*)

noun an important time during an event (*The **highlight** of the birthday party was the cake.*)

Holocaust (**hah** luh **kahst**)

noun the murder of six million Jews by Hitler during World War II (*Many Jewish children lost their parents during the **Holocaust**.*)

noun total or near total destruction of life (*Nuclear weapons can cause a **holocaust**.*)

Ii

illustrate (**il** uh **strayt**)

verb to draw pictures for a book, to explain (*The facts about the Indian Removal Act **illustrate** that Native Americans were treated unfairly.*)

immigration (**im** uh **gray** shuhn)

noun the act of moving into a new country (***Immigration** brought millions of people to America from other countries.*)

imperialism (im **pihr** ee uhl **iz** uhm)

noun a belief that a strong nation builds and controls colonies (*Britain believed in **imperialism** so it controlled colonies in Africa and Asia.*)

import (im **pawt**)

verb to buy products from other countries (*Americans **import** oil from the Middle East for their cars.*)

noun   an item bought from other countries (Americans receive **imports** from all over the world.)

indentured (in **dehn** chuhrd)
adjective   a person who pays off a debt working for free (**Indentured** servants had to work for many years to pay off their debts.)

independence (in dee **pehn** duhns)
noun   the state of being free from outside control (The United States fought for **independence** so it would be free from British rule.)

indicate (in di **kayt**)
verb   to show some kind of fact (Kiri's frown **indicated** that she was unhappy.)

inform (in **fahrm**)
verb   to tell someone facts or to share information (Gustavo's job was to **inform** the government about anyone who committed treason.)

integration (in tuh **gray** shuhn)
noun   to join together people of different races (**Integration** allowed African Americans and whites to sit together in southern restaurants.)

interchangeable (in tuhr **chan** juh buhl)
adjective   something that can be used in place of something else (The words textile and cloth are **interchangeable**.)

internment (in **turn** muhnt)
noun   the act of forcing people to stay in one place, such as a prison or guarded space (Jails are used for the **internment** of criminals.)

intolerance (in **tahl** uhr uhns)
noun   disrespect for others and their beliefs (Mark showed **intolerance** about the beliefs of others.)

isolationism (**eye** suh **lay** shuhn iz **uhm**)
noun   a nation's decision to not get involved with other countries (The United States believed in **isolationism** and stayed out of the war at first.)

Jj

judicial (joo **dish** uhl)
adjective   having to do with the courts and judges (Judges in the **judicial** system make decisions based on the Constitution.)

Ll

legislate (**lej** is **layt**)
verb   to make and pass laws (Congress **legislated** new laws to protect the rights of people with disabilities.)

liberation (lib uhr **ay** shuhn)
noun   the act of freeing people (American soldiers took charge of the **liberation** of the death camps.)

Loyalist (**loy** uh list)
noun   a person who remains loyal to a government, or someone who was loyal to Great Britain during the American Revolution (**Loyalists** in the colonies remained dedicated to Great Britain.)

Mm

manufacturing (**man** yoo **fak** chuhr ing)
noun   the process of making goods in a factory (Textile **manufacturing** saved the seamstress a lot of time.)

verb   making goods in a factory (The factory only **manufactured** popular goods.)

mercantilism (**mur** kuhn til **iz** uhm)
noun   a theory that a nation must sell more products than it buys to be wealthy and strong (**Mercantilism** made England begin to export goods to other nations.)

mercenary (**mur** suh **nehr** ee)
noun   a soldier who fights for pay (The **mercenary** was paid to stay longer with the army.)

migration (my **gray** shuhn)
noun   movement of people or animals from one area to another (In the 1800s there was a large **migration** of people from Europe to America.)

militarism (mil uh tuh **riz** uhm)

noun the building of a powerful military that can be used for war *(Militarism in Germany gave that nation a huge powerful army.)*

militia (muh **lish** uh)

noun an army made up of citizens, not soldiers *(The militia began recruiting friends and neighbors.)*

missionary (mish uhn **ehr** ee)

noun a religious teacher *(The students gathered around the missionary to hear his prayer.)*

mobilize (moh buh **lyz)**

verb to prepare an army for war, or to organize support for a cause *(The United States mobilized thousands of soldiers to fight in World War I.)*

Nn

nationalism (nash uh nuhl **iz** uhm)

noun strong love for one's country and feeling it is better than others *(Our feelings of nationalism were evident as we hung a flag in our yard.)*

nativist (nay tiv ist)

noun someone who is against people arriving from other countries moving in *(Anne was a nativist who did not want foreign people to move to America.)*

neutral (noo truhl)

adjective a nation that does not help or support any fighting nation in a war *(Spain was neutral during World War I and did not fight.)*

nuclear (noo klee uhr)

adjective the huge amount of energy that is given off by splitting atoms *(Nuclear weapons contain very powerful bombs.)*

Oo

objective (uhb jehk tiv)

noun a purpose or goal *(Huong's objective was to become a physician.)*

omit (oh **mit**)

verb to leave out or not include *(I was sad because Mom omitted the sprinkles when she baked cupcakes.)*

organize (awr guh nyz)

verb to put into order *(Yen organized a group to protest the new rules.)*

Pp

patriot (pay tree uht)

noun a person who loves his or her country, or an American colonist who fought for independence *(Thomas Jefferson was a patriot who worked hard for American independence.)*

petition (puh **tish** uhn)

noun a written request *(The student wrote a petition that requested a class trip to Washington, D.C.)*

verb to make a request *(The student petitioned the principal for a class trip to Washington, D.C.)*

pilgrim (pil gruhm)

noun a person who moves or travels to another place for religious reasons *(A group of pilgrims came to America in search of freedom.)*

pioneer (py uh **nihr)**

noun one of the first people of a group to settle in an area, or to do something *(The first people to travel to the moon were pioneers.)*

verb to be one of the first people to do something *(American pioneering on the land near the Mississippi River led to the growth of new towns.)*

plantation (plan **tay** shuhn)

noun a very large farm where crops are grown to be sold *(Al of the goods at the market were grown on the same plantation.)*

portray (pawr **tray**)

verb to show a person, thing, or event in a certain way *(Stories about George Washington portray him as strong, brave leader.)*

predict (pree **dikt**)
   verb   to guess what might happen *(There was no way to **predict** how violent the rebellion would be.)*

progressive (proh **grehs** iv)
   noun   someone who wants to improve society *(The **progressives** came up with a plan to keep the city safe.)*

Prohibition (proh uh **bish** uhn)
   noun   the time during which something popular is made illegal, or the period in the United States when alcoholic beverages were illegal *(During **Prohibition**, people could not buy wine in a store.)*

propaganda (prahp uh **gan** duh)
   noun   ideas spread to change people's opinions about someone or something *(**Propaganda** posters can change people's opinions.)*

propose (pruh **pohz**)
   verb   to suggest a plan *(The students **proposed** that the school calendar include more field trips.)*

proprietor (pruh **pry** uh tuhr)
   noun   a person who owns land or a business *(The **proprietor** was making a good living renting out his land.)*

Qq

quota (**kwoht** uh)
   noun   the number that is a goal, like a limit on the number of immigrants or how many items should be made or sold *(The **quota** system allowed more people to come to America from Britain than Poland.)*

Rr

rebellion (ri **behl** yuhn)
   noun   the act of fighting against the government or the people in charge *(The unfair law caused a **rebellion**.)*

reconstruction (ree kuhn **struhk** shuhn)
   noun   a period of rebuilding, or the rebuilding of the South after the Civil War *(During **Reconstruction**, cities were rebuilt in the South.)*

region (**ree** juhn)
   noun   a large area of similar land *(The southwest is a dry desert **region**.)*

relate (ri **layt**)
   verb   to feel connected to or to respond to something *(Jenny **related** to her neighbor's problems after a fire destroyed the neighbor's home.)*

relief (ri **leef**)
   noun   help for serious problems *(The government created thousands of jobs to give **relief** to the jobless.)*

removal (ri **moo** vuhl)
   noun   the act of taking away, or moving away *(During the winter, snow **removal** makes driving safer.)*

reparation (rehp uh **ray** shuhn)
   noun   money that a nation that has lost a war must pay the winning countries *(Germany was required to pay **reparations** to France and other countries after World War I.)*

repeal (ri **peel**)
   verb   to end or remove a law *(The people wanted to **repeal** the new tax law.)*

representative (rehp ruh **zehn** tuh tiv)
   noun   a person who is elected to make laws in Congress, or a person who acts for other people *(**Representatives** are elected to serve two year terms in the House of Representatives.)*

republic (ri **puhb** lik)
   noun   a country in which citizens vote for government leaders *(The United States is a **republic** because Americans vote for their President and lawmakers.)*

respond (ri **spahnd**)
   verb   to do or say something about what was done or said *(I told my sister that I wanted a birthday party and she **responded** with a surprise!)*

retaliation (ri **tal** ee **ay** shuhn)
   noun   the act of taking action against a person or country that has hurt you *(In 1941 the United States went to war against Japan in **retaliation** for the bombing of Pearl Harbor.)*